THE RELUCTANT ROAD WARRIOR

The adventures of a Silicon Valley engineer in the U.S. and abroad

Dan P. Bullard

To April, Christopher, Candice and Samantha.

I couldn't have done it without you.

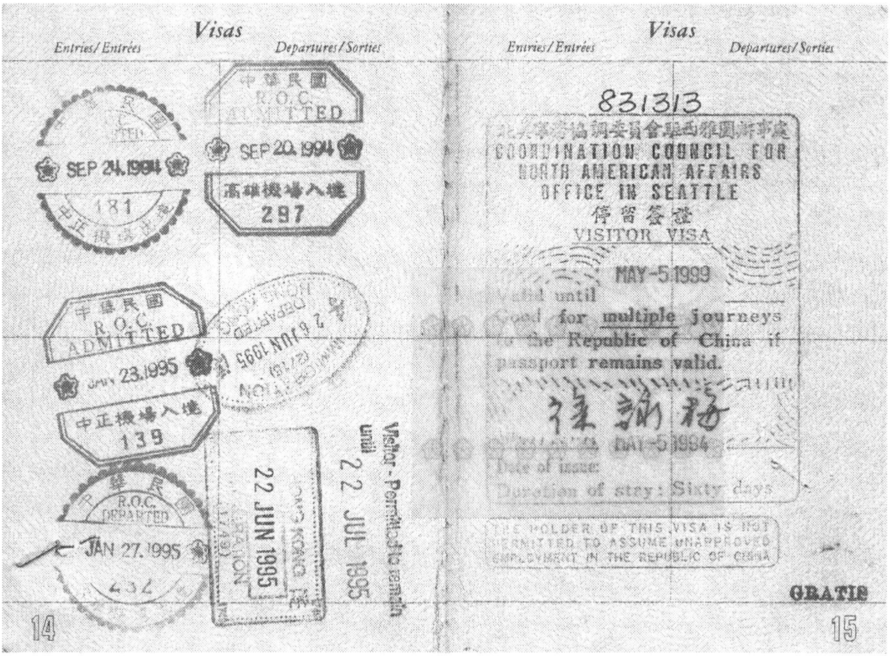

Life is like the coldest winter
People will freeze the tears I cry
Words of hail their minds are into
I've got to crack this ice and fly
Gonna hitch a ride
Head for the other side
Leave it all behind
Never change my mind
Gonna sail away
Sun lights another day
Freedom on my mind
Carry me away for the last time
Hitch A Ride by Boston

The Reluctant Road Warrior

The adventures of a Silicon Valley engineer in the U.S. and abroad

By Dan P. Bullard

ISBN-13: 978-1523900077
ISBN-10: 1523900075
DDC 609
Business travel, humor, semiconductors

Cover art: Collage of photos from Dan's travels on a background of Dan's passport stamps.

Other books by Dan P. Bullard
Distortion: The Cause Of Harmonics And The Lie Of THD

Learn more about Dan at www.danbullard.com

Forward

This book is a compilation of memories of events I experienced as I traveled around the world saving the day (or not in some cases) trying to keep machines humming along, producing semiconductor devices that went into PCs, fighter planes, cell phones, cars, guided missiles, toys, wireless internet, and millions of other electronic do-dads. Don't fret though, no electronics knowledge is required to follow the stories contained herein. Don't be surprised if you learn something though. I am a trainer by trade after all.

While I fictionalized all names and details of many events to protect the innocent and guilty alike, it's quite possible that someone will recognize themselves in these stories. My memories may be different from those of the people I worked with, and if they have any complaints I expect that problem can be addressed by writing their own story. No attempt to defame, libel or slander was made while writing this book. As you will see, much alcohol was consumed and might be responsible for differences in the perception of the events contained in this book.

Some people have different skills than others. There was a reason I was sent to these, in some cases, Godforsaken places: Because all the other people who had tried to solve the problem were unable to, I was sent in. Lucky me! It's not my fault I have a gift for troubleshooting electronics better than most "degreed" engineers. My degree came from the school of hard knocks, and as you will see, at times it was a grueling education. I apologize in advance to anyone who was there and feels that I took more credit than I deserved. Let's face it, you couldn't have done it without me, no matter how much effort you contributed. Of course, everyone is the hero of his own story. This is my story. True or not, I am the hero in this book.

Part of the reason I wrote this book was to address comments from various friends and family members who thought I was one of those *rich pampered egghead paper-pushers*, who lived high on the hog on a limitless expense account. Obviously I was too highly paid for no good reason and deserved to be taxed until my income was equal to theirs. I was well paid, at my peak I earned up to $150,000 a year, not counting stock options and bonuses. I unashamedly enjoyed spending the portion of that money Uncle Sam "allowed" me to keep. Most of those people are dead now, but plenty of people still think that money comes easily to those who have it. Not even close!

This book will expose the reason why those of us who travel for a living are so highly paid, and how we **earn** every dime of it. You can earn that kind of money too, if after reading this book you are still willing to get on a plane bound for God-knows-where to do God-knows-what for God-knows-how-long working for God-knows-who and endure every bacteria, virus, toxin, gas and strange semi-edible creature known to humanity. You can come home when the maniacal, power-crazed customer says you can, or maybe just be sent to the next hellhole as means of payment for a job well done. This is my story, and I'm a proud of what I accomplished, but I am oh so glad it's over!

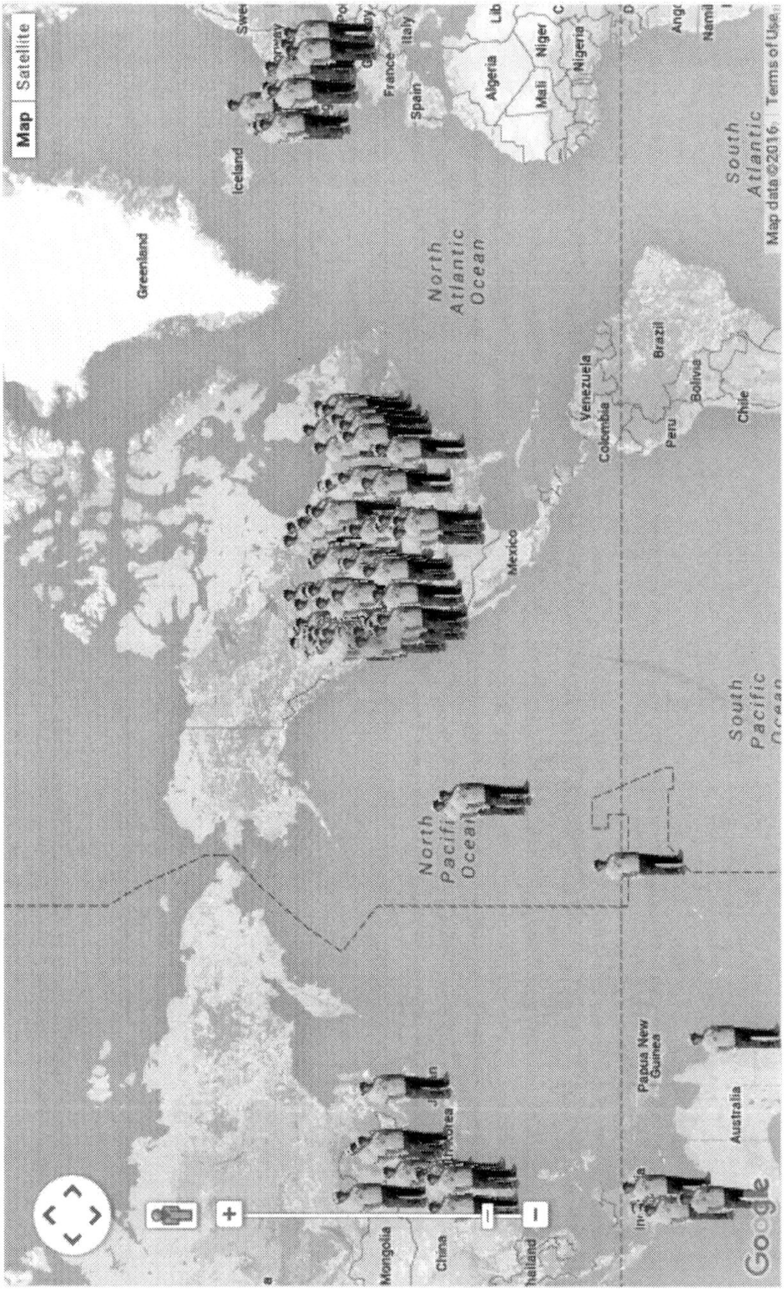

www.danbullard.com/dan/dans_travels.html

Table of Contents

A note on organization

Rather than drone on and on about my travels in straight chronological fashion, I have broken up this book into chapters based on the region I was traveling to. If you have no interest in Kokomo, or Texas, or Taiwan, you are free to skip those chapters. However, be warned that some of the funniest things happened in the most unlikely places, you never know what you are going to miss. You can always read a chapter you skipped because the timeline is not crucial here.

Each chapter proceeds more or less chronologically, with a few instances of time hopping as needed to make sure everything makes sense. Because of this organization, every chapter starts by rewinding back to my earliest days in the semiconductor test industry, and then proceeds through the years to end at my last visit to that region. What I think is really great about this organization is that even though I changed companies a lot, and because the semiconductor industry is such a small, specialized group of people, the same folks keep popping up again and again in different places and in different companies around the world.

I hope you don't get too confused because to make things even more interesting, in the middle of my career I moved from San Jose, California to Beaverton, Oregon, near Portland. In chapter after chapter you'll find that half the time I am flying out of SJC (San Jose International) and then the next thing you know I am flying out of PDX (Portland International). Eventually I will explain how that came about. It's an interesting story in itself.

Enjoy!

Where did that stuff come from?

You have a cell phone. You probably have a car and a computer. A credit card? You watch cable, satellite or streaming TV. You surf the web, listen to music, play video games and talk with, text or message people far away from where you live. One hundred years ago, virtually none of these things were possible. How did they come about? By magic?

The obvious answer is that someone built that stuff, but who? Even though most of that stuff comes out of Asia today, it was all invented in the U.S. and then migrated to Asia, where manufacturing (and life) is cheap.

Brilliant men and women with names like Shockley, Bardeen, Brattain, Noyce, Moore, Amdahl, Gates, Jobs, Vollum, Mees, Gifford, Lamarr, Healy and tens of thousands of others whose accomplishments might not have been great enough to get them a place in the history books, made the world better by their sweat, their perseverance and their work ethic.

All of these men and women helped build the world we have today, and if any one of them had not come through, it would have put us behind. Maybe a week, maybe a year, maybe an eternity. Shockley, Bardeen and Brattain invented the transistor. Without them, we might still be using vacuum tubes. The Hollywood actress Hedy Lamarr invented Spread Spectrum radio communications to create a jam-proof radio system to aid the war effort during WWII. Today Spread Spectrum is used in cell phones, Bluetooth, GPS, wireless internet, etcetera. Could we live without it? Not really. There are not enough frequencies in the radio spectrum for everyone to have his own personal radio channel. Lamarr's invention allows billions of people to talk at the same time using only a very narrow RF spectrum.

Nameless engineers did their part in bringing all this stuff to fruition. They got up in the morning, worked for 8, 10, 14, 18, sometimes 24 hours to write code, design hardware, collect data, fix stuff and do a thousand things that just needed to get done. When they couldn't take it anymore they would go home, try to unwind from these very draining activities, then get up the next morning and do it all again. I was one of those nameless engineers.

It was an exciting time. We didn't know we were building the future. We were just trying to pay the rent, keep the cars running, keep food in the stomachs of our spouse and children and save for the day when we could give it all up and rest before the slings and arrows of this hard life put us in the ground for good. Some never crossed that finish line. Many of the smartest and hardest working people I knew died before they could "slow down and live their life full measure."

I was a small part of this giant human machine. Now I ask you to follow me around the world and understand what thousands of us went through to make it all happen. We did it for ourselves, but like every other capitalist enterprise, you are the beneficiary.

Goodbye my love, Maybe for forever
Goodbye my love, The tide waits for me
Who knows when we shall meet again
If ever
But time
Keeps flowing like a river (on and on)
To the sea, to the sea
Time by The Alan Parsons Project

Kokomo

"Ooo I wanna take you down to Kokomo
We'll get there fast
And then we'll take it slow
That's where we wanna go
Way down to Kokomo"
Kokomo by the Beach Boys

For the uninitiated, Kokomo is not some magical place in the Florida Keys. It's a small rust belt town a couple of hours north of Indianapolis, Indiana. In the 1980s there were two places you could get a decent paying job in Kokomo; the Chrysler Transmission plant, or just across Highway 31, the Gizmotronics plant, a division of OMG. In 1986 it was my misfortune to be sent to Kokomo to deliver the first of several RadChek RC16 maintenance training courses for some of the Gizmotronics employees. The course was three weeks long at the time, which is a long time to be away from home, especially when there is a wife and two little kids at home. No matter, this is what the boss wanted, this is what the salesperson wanted and this is what the customer wanted so that is where I was going to go, *way down to Kokomo.*

I had never taken a business trip before and my boss, George Gregory tried to convince me it would be great. He told me that the company would pay for *everything*. Big mistake, as he would find out when I submitted my expense report, but back to the story.

We packed all the manuals, RadChek embossed coffee cups, the works and shipped them to the local RadChek office in Kokomo. The office had a classroom and a RadCheck RC16 tester! I was to find this was seldom the case on other trips, but this was a good way to start for sure. The company travel office made the arrangements to get me to Indianapolis so all I had to do was catch the plane, then grab my rental car at Indianapolis and drive up Highway 31 to Kokomo. I had a room at the Ramada so I was set.

The standard plan was to fly in on Sunday and start class on Monday. So Sunday night I flew in, drove to Kokomo, found the hotel and checked in. I was able to find a grocery store so I could stock up on my favorite adult beverage at the time, Budweiser, but when I walked past the clerk and mentioned I was there to buy some beer she said, "Not on Sunday!" I was astounded to find that not every state was like California, you couldn't buy beer on Sunday, not in Indiana. The beer coolers had tape over them so you couldn't get in. I was shocked! What is this going to be like spending nearly a month in a place where you can't just buy beer anytime you feel like it?

Now I was concerned. I was able to buy a beer back at the hotel bar, but they were only open till 10PM, so I had to drink fast having arrived at 9PM.

At the RadChek office the next morning I met the staff and found them to be very helpful. They had gotten my boxes of manuals (about 40 pounds of books per person) and had them ready for me to lay out in the classroom which was in the basement of the building. The students started showing up, dressed in rather casual attire which surprised me. I wore my standard attire, slacks, a long sleeve dress shirt and a tie. When everyone was there I was able to start teaching right away and things went well.

After a while though, I started getting this odd attitude from the students. I had never dealt with union members and these guys were hard-core union boys. They joked about me being from California, as in, "Don't ever bend over in front of a Californian" as though everyone from California was queer (the vernacular at the time). I tried not to take it personally but it did grate on me. Still, these were customers, so you can't give them grief. We sold them quite a few RC16 testers, at something like $400,000 each, whereas my salary was about $35,000 a year. I was a nobody, I knew it and more importantly *they knew it*. I put up with it because I had to spend the next three weeks with these guys and there were three mouths to feed, clothe and house back home, so what else could I do?

Since teaching the class only took nine hours a day, I had to find a way to occupy myself the other fifteen hours a day. Much of that was sleeping, and much of that was drinking. I did have an additional assignment to complete in my "off" time. RadChek rented a furnished apartment to be used by visiting trainers, applications engineers and the salesperson, a woman whom I never met. Since I was the first visiting "dignitary" it was my job to outfit this place, then move in when it was ready. I had to shop for things like shower curtains, pots and pans, plates and glasses, sheets and blankets. Brandi, the receptionist at the RadChek office helped me some, but mostly I did it on my own. Within a week I had the place outfitted and moved out of the Ramada into my new "bachelor pad." I had gotten an advance on my expense account to pay for all this stuff, and was assured that the company would pay for it. I was not very thrifty with the money, since it wasn't mine. That turned out to be a mistake later. One weekend I ended up buying a fishing pole and tackle (the company is paying, right?) and took off fishing at one of the many nearby lakes. It was kind of a pretty place after you got use to the lack of mountains. It wasn't much like being home, but I could survive it. So I taught by day and like a good married man away from home, drank beer and slept alone by night.

At one point during the training, Brandi informed me that Corporate forgot to pay the water bill for the office and that the water in the facility was going to be shut off. My students pitched in, bringing barrels and buckets of water in the beds of their pickup trucks so we could flush the toilets. I took a fair bit of ribbing about that from the students. They wanted to know what RadChek was doing with all the money Gizmotronics was spending on testers and why we couldn't afford to keep the water turned on. Bastards.

One day when I dismissed the class to go to lunch and was getting ready to go out with Brandi and the staff, Brandi got a phone call from her son, David, who was stationed in West Germany with the Army. He had a new baby and wanted Grandma to hear the baby cry. She was so excited she tried to record the call on the answering machine. After the call she checked for the recorded audio, but couldn't seem to find it. Oh well, she thought, she could look for it after we got back from lunch. We all went off together and came back to hear a strange message on the answering machine. It seems that Brandi *was* successful in recording all this commotion on the answering machine, but onto the *outgoing message*. So, when an engineer from Gizmotronics called at lunchtime to complain about a system being down, instead of hearing a businesslike greeting such as "Thank you for calling RadChek Kokomo, we can't take your call right now, please leave a message," he heard:

"whaaaa, whaaa, whaaaaaaa!...Goddamn baby cries all the fucking time!...David you watch your mouth, especially around that baby!"

The caller was more than a little confused. She was a nice lady, but technology was not her strong suit.

Finally graduation day came. I got the students to fill out the critiques, thanked them and sent them on their way. I was eager to get home to my little sweetie. Before I left, one of the RadChek guys asked me why I didn't graduate the class, claiming that the students were a little upset about it. "Why do they think that I didn't pass them?" I asked. *"Because you didn't give them diplomas!"* he exclaimed. Oh shit, I forgot about the diplomas! Every vendor gave out diplomas after a class, and I had totally forgotten them. I made a quick call back to San Jose and put in an order for diplomas to be made up, I would sign them when I got back on Monday and we could mail them back to Kokomo to be handed out. In the meantime I asked all the staff to inform the students that they *were* getting diplomas, they were just delayed. I had to come up with a way to produce them locally in the future, and this was long before laptops, so it was going to be tricky. I simply hoped that this time the students (customers) weren't going to rush back to work and complain to their management, or worse yet, the Union, that a deviate Californian had made them sit in class for three weeks and then failed them. In the end it all worked out, Gizmotronics forgave me, and that meant I got to do more classes! Yay?

When I got back to San Jose I started on my expense report. This turned out to be a nightmare, there were many things that I bought that the company would NOT reimburse me for, like the fishing pole. I had to justify every item, from shower curtains to drinking glasses to laundry detergent. It was a real pain. After complaining to George, George's boss, Pat Anthony just grabbed my expense report and made a note, claiming $200 in lost receipts. That was good enough for me, but I sure learned a lesson.

Despite what most of my liberal friends and family think, being on an expense account isn't an excuse to pamper yourself foolishly with the company's money. While a few of my coworkers did cheat on their figures some to pay for drinking or worse, it was hard to get away with much. One guy I worked with got a nasty letter from the CFO for an 18 cent phone charge. I became a stickler for the facts, too afraid that someone might challenge me on my numbers and get me fired for stealing from the company.

A few weeks after being home the wife noticed a gray hair in my head. A gray hair at age 30! She plucked it from my head and I mailed it to Brandi, telling her that it was Kokomo's fault I was getting gray hairs. Of course it was a joke, albeit a mean one, but it was funny!

My next trip to Kokomo was slightly better. A RadChek employee in the area, an older German fellow named Adolf suggested that I try staying at one of the rental condos on Morse Lake in the tiny town of Cicero. This place was sweet! My own deck right on the lake, a fireplace with complementary fire log every night, cable TV, what a place! It also had maid service, unlike my apartment in Kokomo. The only downside was that it was a 45 minute drive from Kokomo, but life here was at least bearable, if still lonely.

On my next trip I came up with a solution to the loneliness. The class had now been lengthened to four weeks after we added a week long module on maintaining the computer subsystem. RadChek had a policy that allowed you to fly home after two weeks if your trip was four or more weeks long. I asked if it would be possible to fly my wife, April out instead and let her stay with me at the condo in Cicero. We had a new baby daughter at the time, but April could bring her along, and the older kids could stay with my parents in the mountains near West Point, California. My boss got the OK from management and we were set. I flew out to Kokomo, spent two weeks

teaching, then drove down to Indianapolis to pick up April and baby at the airport. Then we hit a snag. The airline lost her luggage. They promised to find it and ship it up to Cicero when they did, which happened a couple of days later. April had a wonderful time there. She blended right in with the townsfolk, walking the baby around in the stroller while I spent the days teaching. It was a glorious week. One night we were having dinner at a local restaurant and the baby started crying. A waitress grabbed her from April and walked off into the kitchen so we could enjoy our dinner. That didn't work out too well, as April was nervous about letting a stranger in a town thousands of miles from home walk off with her new baby, and the chef in the kitchen got pissed off at having a crying baby making a ruckus in his workspace.

One day April came to Kokomo with me so she could spend the day with Brandi, as we were old friends by now, and she did love babies, even crying ones and as I mentioned, my newborn daughter was a wailer.

I was getting increasingly frustrated with the union guys I was having to train. A few days earlier, the guys in the class asked me if I possessed a cabling diagram for the tester. I had to admit that I didn't, but that they should be able to figure it out based on the other documents I had given them. The tester must have contained a couple hundred cables, and we all know they aren't going to spontaneously unplug themselves. When I asked why they needed such a diagram for this behemoth of a machine the answer was this: When the Union calls a strike, all the electricians sabotage the systems by de-cabling them before walking out the door. They needed the diagram to be able to put the tester back together after the strike was over. I was *stunned*, how awful! How vengeful! How WRONG! I promised them that they would be able to re-cable the system by the time the class was over in a week.

So, on this day while my wife is in the lobby making coffee before class and Brandi is cuddling the baby, I am in the demo room which had only a glass wall between the tester and the lobby. As my wife and some of the early arriving students watched in delight and horror (respectively) I yanked cables from the backplanes, tossed them over the tester onto the floor and de-cabled the whole beast right before their eyes. I had already pulled every circuit board from the tester, carried them downstairs to the basement and piled them on the students desks. The tester was now fully gutted. Who's the bastard now? The rest of the students arrived and I told them that the strike was over and it was time to put the tester back together. It was vengeful, but also very instructive. At first the students were a bit pissed off at me, but I worked with them and guided them through the job and by the end of the day, we had the tester back up, calibrated and running diagnostics. They learned a valuable lesson, not just about the tester, but also about arrogance and retribution. I objected to their attitude towards their employer, and now they knew it and had to respect it. A week later I got the critiques, not one negative comment about my stunt, they all seemed to enjoy the class. I was pleased, and relieved! Shockingly, no future Gizmotronics students ever asked for a cabling diagram. I wonder if the word had gotten out to the factory.

We never had any Gizmotronics union people come to training in San Jose because union rules stated that Gizmotronics would have to pay them for every minute they were away from home, don't I wish! However we did get a visit from one Richard Cadillac, a nonunion engineer from Kokomo. He was quite infamous with the RadChek people servicing Kokomo, a real prick they said. He came out to San Jose for a System Administrators training class, which I would normally have taught, but my new boss Sylvester Sloan took it over for me since Richard was the only student, and I had been "on platform" almost continuously for months. I told Sylvester that I was working on a Random Number Generator, which he assumed had something to do with the Algorithmic Pattern Generator in the tester, so he let me off the hook. Instead, I was *really* working on a linear congruential random number generator to use in my new game program called Slots, a slot machine simulator that turned out to be very popular with RadChek employees and customers alike. I loved writing Pascal programs and it helped me learn many computer science concepts that I would need to understand if I was going to teach Pascal with any authority. Besides it was fun!

Richard was true to his name, he could be a real dick, but of course as the advocate for Gizmotronics, he had to take a superior attitude towards us, his vendor. Richard really pissed me off when he asked me for my last remaining copy of the VT100 programming guide, my bible and my own personal copy. I gave it up, but later he returned it after he felt bad for taking it from me. I would run into Richard on another trip to Kokomo, but this time things would be different.

This next trip was going to be a breeze, I was only going to have to teach the first week of the class, with Roary Gay, an old-time tech support guy flying in Friday to take over the last three weeks. Also, the class was run during the swing shift, from 3PM to 11PM. The biggest change was that it was going to be on site, at Gizmotronics. I had heard about the Gizmotronics plant, but had never been there. I was concerned, and as it turns out, for good reason.

I shipped the manuals to Brandi and on Monday morning I met her at the office to get the manuals and move them to Gizmotronics. We piled the boxes into the back of her Floored pickup and drove to Gizmotronics separately. I parked my car in the visitor parking, and then waited for Brandi to get through the guarded gate at Gizmotronics. It seemed to take forever, and when she did arrive with the boxes she told me what kept her. It seems that a Floored pickup is not an OMG product, and company rules say no non-OMG vehicles are allowed on site. After going round and round with the guard, he finally found someone who would authorize it *this time*. Petty bullshit always pisses me off. So now we get to the loading dock to unload the boxes so they can get to the classroom, but *we can't unload them*. Union rules say that only union guys can unload boxes and we got even more crap because these union guys had to *touch* a Floored pickup to get to the boxes. Worse yet, these guys can't take them to the classroom. This huge plant is divided up into sectors, and these guys can only take the boxes to the edge of this sector, then leave the boxes there. When and if the next sector's guys find them, they will take them as far as the next sector boundary and leave them, and so on and so on. Eventually the boxes will get to our classroom, but will they get there by 3PM for the start of class? No guarantees pal! Great.

When 3PM came I made it to the classroom and met the students, but there were no boxes! The manuals had not found their way to the classroom. I told the guys the story and several of them left and came back with the boxes! They risked union sanctions and carried the boxes of manuals themselves, but since they were engineers and not "box carriers" they could have gotten in trouble with the union guys. No matter, these guys wanted to learn and that attitude helped *my* attitude immensely. We had a good time for the next few days.

I learned a lot about union life. To get to the classroom I had to walk through one of the machine shops. Every time I walked through the shop the machinists there were either playing cards, reading books or just gone, screwing off somewhere else. I never saw them use any of the machine tools; lathes, milling machines, drill presses, etcetera in the shop. Mostly what they used there were the chairs to sit on their lazy asses.

On my final day there, I taught the class about the Phoenix hard drive and prepared them for the head alignment procedure that we would perform after dinner. We went out to a classy restaurant for our class dinner and drank way too much. Now we had to *do* the disk drive head alignment, a very sensitive and potentially dangerous procedure if you do it wrong. You could destroy the hard drive, or get seriously injured if you put too much pressure on the head actuator, and we are all too drunk to drive, let alone align and torque a hard drive head flying at a microscopic distance over a rapidly spinning disk. It's a wonder we didn't get somebody hurt, but everyone took a turn and all survived, including the hard drive.

Then as we were wrapping up, Roary Gay arrived. He had just flown in and driven up from Indianapolis. I wanted Roary to be there on Friday evening even though he didn't have to start teaching until Monday so I could fill him in on all the procedures, introduce him to the students, etcetera. Of course the first thing out of Roary's mouth was a tirade about the shitty rental car he got. It was a brand new Shavey Bearetta, made of course by these very guys Roary was going to spend the next three weeks with. Way to win friends Roary.

After class that night some of the guys wanted to go back to drinking, and since my plane didn't leave until the next day I was game. We got seriously hammered and then one of the guys who claimed to have his own airplane decided we should go flying at night! There are a number of places I wouldn't mind dying, but Kokomo, Indiana isn't one of them. I turned him down and got home to my loving wife and family the next day. Better than lying dead in a cornfield in Indiana next to a drunk pilot.

My final trip to Kokomo was in a totally different capacity. I was teaching the applications training course by now, having graduated to writing software instead of spinning screwdrivers. This was a special class: Gizmotronics had bought a new option for the RadChek testers, an interactive graphical "oscilloscope" tool with a mouse and everything! This would let you observe the signals that the tester was sending to the DUT, Device (or chip) Under Test *and* to see the signals the chip was sending back. I developed the three day class using one of Gizmotronics's own chips and a program that RadChek wrote for them, which would make the class much more relevant to them.

There was one feature of the test program for this chip that the Gizmotronics guys couldn't quite comprehend, it was called Match Mode. This mode allows the tester to loop on a pattern until the chip "matches" or passes a test. As long as the pattern fails to match the expected pattern, it would continue to loop, trying again, and again and again. When the test finally passes, the tester drops out of the loop and continues on to complete the rest of the testing. Yeah, they didn't understand it either.

Another interesting wrinkle, my old buddy Richard Cadillac was in the class. *Oh brother* I thought, but what the heck, it was only three days. I gave the class and on the last day, I used this graphical debug tool to show them how the match mode loop worked. They were blown away, they all understood it now, it made perfect sense looking at it on this fancy new tool they had bought. As I passed out the training critique forms to the students, Richard asked me for one. He said, "I have never felt the need to fill one of these out before, but I can't resist after what I just saw!" What I got was a glowing review from Richard, it was among my most prized possessions at RadChek.

Now if you're feelin' kinda low 'bout the dues you've been paying
Future's coming much too slow
And you wanna run but somehow you just keep on stayin'
Can't decide on which way to go
Yeah, yeah, yeah

I understand about indecision
But I don't care if I get behind
People livin' in competition
All I want is to have my peace of mind.

Now you're climbin' to the top of the company ladder
Hope it doesn't take too long
Can'tcha see there'll come a day when it won't matter
Come a day when you'll be gone
Peace Of Mind by Boston

Boston

"Go away, we are working!"
Axmi engineer's response when I introduced myself as the new trainer.

Just about the time I left RadChek and joined Steppenwolf, the parent company, Semiconductor Ossification Systems (SOS) bought a small mixed signal tester company in Burlington Massachusetts named Axmi. The Axmi AX100 was an odd machine and no one at SOS knew anything about it, but my old boss George from RadChek who had moved to SOS before me told me that mixed signal was the *wave of the future*. Kind of a play on words because mixed signal involves waves more than digital test does. George had never steered me wrong. Well, except in the area of expense reports on my first Kokomo trip, but I was game and it seemed very interesting. Problem was, I had to work with a group of people back in Massachusetts who were not happy about being bought out by a California company (too many sexual deviants you know).

Because the woman I replaced, Sally Struther had quit a month before I came on board, SOS hired a contractor named Zieg Roberts who previously worked for Axmi, but had since retired to a Buddhist commune in Nova Scotia. His job was to train me on this new mixed signal tester in San Jose. We had two customers from Southern Morse who had signed up for training, so the class wasn't just for me. The instructor was kind of a jerk.

For example, during a lecture on Sampling Theory, Zieg asked the class for a number for *N*, the number of samples to capture during a test. I volunteered a value of 1000. Zieg said, "OK" and went with that number for the calculations for his example. Problem was that 1000 is not a valid value for *N* according to the software. It expects *N* to be two to the power of some integer, so 2 to the power of 10 (2*2*2*2*2*2*2*2*2*2), or 1024 would be allowed, but 1000 would not be. He should have told me that during the lecture because that is what instructors are supposed to do when students blurt out the wrong answer. Because he didn't correct me I thought 1000 was a valid value to use. Then lab time came. I tried to use 1000 but the software kept fighting me without giving me a good explanation of what I was doing wrong. Finally Zeig told me I could not use 1000, it has to be a power of two, like 1024. Why not tell me during the lecture? See what I mean? A real jerk.

What nagged me even more was the fact that I couldn't seem to get much help from headquarters in Burlington. However there was a class coming up in Burlington for some customers and two Sicas employees, another acquisition, and I would be able to meet the Axmi crew and try to get some face to face training.

I flew out to Boston and arrived late in the day. I thought I was well prepared for the trip but after I got out of Boston proper I got lost, very, very lost. I drove for hours looking for my hotel, and finally found it, around 9PM. It was a very opulent hotel, The Guest Quarters, very much like an Embassy Suites.

The next day I found my way to the office and started meeting people. I had a week to prepare for the class so I got to work trying to make new friends by walking around introducing myself. The people ranged from warm to just downright rude. When I went into a laboratory and introduced myself to these two guys they told me, “Go away, we are working.” That was Al Levinvich, a nasty Russian guy and Ned Ryerson, one of the software engineers. Later Al would suck up to me when he needed a job and got the cold shoulder because that was what he gave me on my first trip out to Boston.

However some people were OK. Malcolm Reynolds who would later move out to Oregon and become a good friend started out by giving me a puzzle. He walked up to me, unbuttoned the top button in my shirt, jammed some kind of stick and string puzzle through the button hole in my shirt and walked away to see if I could solve it. After a few minutes, I gave up and he had his answer. I was not as smart has he had hoped. Later, I would find a way to save face, but this was not a good way to start.

Will Charlatan, the one and only Axmi field service engineer was quite friendly, in an East Coast sort of way. He introduced me to the technical publications writer, Andy Mayberry. Andy is black, one of two black guys at Axmi. Andy had served in the U.S. Air Force, so we got along quite well, trading stories about the service and the places we had been stationed. Will invited me to join him and Andy for lunch, so we went out to the parking lot and Will unlocked the doors on his Dodge Caravan. I expected to have to ride in the back seat, but Andy slid the side door open and sat way in the back seat. I told him, “Andy, you don’t have to sit in the back of the bus anymore,” a rather pointed comment about his race. I knew I had judged him properly when he chuckled and told me that he preferred the back seat because he was nearly 7 feet tall and the back seat gave him more leg room than the front seat of the mini-van. Andy was right, this Caravan was stingy on leg room even for a guy like me at 6 feet tall.

I needed to learn as much as I could while I was there, but I also needed to setup a classroom. I was told there was a conference room that I could use, but I couldn't use it all the time. There were high level meetings scheduled in there from time to time and I would occasionally get kicked out. This was not going to work so I started looking around the building. I found a makeshift storeroom packed with junk; boxes, old furniture and other stuff, but its use was uncontested so I decided to see if I could clear it out enough to use as a classroom. After a couple of hours Will came looking for me and after I told him what I had in mind he decided to help me out. We used some old office partition walls to wall off an area in the back for the junk we couldn't use and I was able to scrounge up 5 desks and an equal number of chairs. We wired it for terminals, put up a white board, and TA-DA! I had a classroom that no one would kick me out of!

The class was going to be taught partly by me and partly by Zieg, the contractor we had used in San Jose. I knew that the two guys from Sicas were digital only but at least they did know test and they knew UNIX which was used on this tester. I was lucky that the tester used the same version of Pascal (Oregon Pascal coincidentally as it turns out) that I was used to on the RadChek testers. UNIX was new to me, but I learned it quickly.

I had a good time co-teaching the class and learned a lot more about this tester. The software was really sweet, well thought out and robust. It seemed like they had thought of just about everything.

One of the guys from Sicas, Dick Holmes, was a competent guy and we got along well and became friends. The other guy, Dexter James, didn't really want to learn mixed signal, he was just there because his boss told him to be there, so we didn't really form much of a friendship.

One week of prep time to build the classroom and try to milk the engineers for information, two weeks for the training class, and then another week for more training, four weeks away from home. It was difficult, but I managed. After two weeks, the hotel wanted to be paid to make sure I didn't skip out on them. I had to pay them $1400 cash, otherwise they would toss me out. I wasn't too fond of being considered a flight risk, but the hotel was rather plush and swanky, so I stayed.

Getting meals in the Burlington area was a bit of a challenge. On the West Coast you can always find a Denny's or Burger King or McDonald's, but on the East Coast it wasn't that easy. On a later trip to Boston I wasn't allowed to stay in the Guest Quarters. Apparently all these company acquisitions drained the bank accounts, so I had to stay in the Woburn Inn. This was a plain-Jane motel like the kind you might use for a lunchtime rendezvous with a female coworker. Unlike the Guest Quarters, it did not have a breakfast buffet or restaurant of any kind. It didn't have a mini-bar fridge either, so if I wanted beer or something that had to be kept cold I had to put it on the window ledge outside my room and use the frigid temperatures to keep it cool.

Breakfast was a nightmare. I found only one place that served breakfast, a greasy spoon with a gravel parking lot and a leaky roof. I remember watching the waitress and the fry cook working hard to fill orders while rainwater leaked from the roof onto the grill sending clouds of steam into the air. I didn't want to think about all the crap on the roof that was being washed into the food on the grill. Yuck!

The training manuals Zieg (Buddha Boy) and Sally (the quitter) created for the class left a lot to be desired. Zieg wasn't a very good trainer nor was he a very good training course developer. Some of the slides he made looked like they belonged in a kindergarten classroom. So I started asking some of the secretaries in the Burlington office if I could use their Macintosh computers after they went home at night. Most were OK with that, so I would do a full day teaching and then spend the evening working on developing new training materials using MacDraw or MacWrite. I started getting good at carrying a floppy disk around in my shirt pocket and finding computer time anywhere I could. It would have been wonderful to have a laptop, but Macintosh laptops were very expensive and although everyone in the company seemed to have a Mac, I was not considered worthy enough to get a Mac on my desk or in my travel bag. I just had to borrow time on other people's Macs.

The Boston area is steeped in history and so on the weekends I would go out and find things to do. I went to Walden Pond, subject of the book by Henry David Thoreau. I was told by the locals that in the summertime Walden Pond is about 90% urine since all the local families go there to swim and the kids would just pee in the water. To ruin the ambience a railroad track ran behind the pond and the occasional train would chug through, ruining the fantasy of wilderness inspired by Thoreau's book.

One very cold day I found a park with a smallish pond that was frozen over solid and spent the day there, all by myself getting blitzed and walking around on the ice looking at the under-ice features of the pond. I was never able to do this in California where I grew up, it was magical. Later I found a really, really big pond and saw some kids ice skating on part of it. So I pulled over, parked my rental car and went for a walk on the ice. I got way, way out before I realized that I was in real danger of falling through the ice and drowning. All the time I had been walking I would hear this occasional "thud." Out in the middle of the lake I finally realized it was the sound of the ice cracking behind me and now I seriously worried about being able to get back to land before I fell through. I moved very slowly to make my way back to my rental car. After a half hour I stepped off the ice and vowed to never, ever get back on ice like that again. Had I fallen through, my coworkers might have reported me missing, my rental car might be found but I would be at the bottom of the lake, not to be found until next spring or summer, or maybe never. I imagined what that would have done to my wife and kids and the thought was just unbearable. No more ice for me!

Speaking of ice, I still found the folks at Axmi a bit cold and distant. Compared to the folks in California, they were hostile. One time I was teaching a training class to a couple of customers at the Axmi office when I got a rather rude surprise. I was showing them how to single step through some program code in the debugger when we came across a curious status message that said, "The Voltmeter is connected to Al Levinvich." This made no sense, it was obviously a bug, someone's humorous attempt to create a placeholder for an uninitialized variable. I thought, well, as embarrassing as this is, I can turn this around and make it positive by sending a bug report to Ned Ryerson, the local software engineer I had (sort of) met on my first day in Burlington. I showed the students how to use the email tool and how to copy the strange message we had gotten and then how to paste it into the email message window. Copy and Paste was a new concept at this time. I sent it, confident that the customers would see this as a positive lesson. A minute later I got a reply from Ned. I exclaimed "Oh, look at that, what service! How great is that?" The reply said: "My boss told me I don't have to help you. Leave me alone, I'm busy." Way to make points you stupid asshole! The customers were stunned that he would be such a jerk! I took a break and went to give him a piece of my mind. Never had I seen such disrespect, and it was bad enough to do that to a coworker, but to do it in front of customers was unacceptable. His response was obvious, he didn't know I had customers with me, but that was unacceptable because the way he had treated me as a coworker was just plain rude.

This kind of thing happened quite frequently, and because of this I learned to be self reliant when it came to the tester and mixed signal. Once in Ireland, I sent a fax to Bob Badas in Burlington asking him to call me at my hotel no earlier than noon **his** time, which would put me in the hotel after class at 5PM **my** time. I needed a few questions answered and I would stay in the room to wait for his call. I could not make an international call from the hotel and this was before email, so a fax sent the night before was the surest way to get the message to him. I waited until midnight, which would be 7PM in Boston and gave up. I was able to get a call into Bob the next day. He said he didn't call me because he didn't want to wake me up. I reminded him that my fax said I would be waiting up to answer his call, so the lack of a call inhibited my sleep. I had waited seven hours for him to call me and he didn't do it because he couldn't figure out how the time zone difference worked. What kind of software engineer can't understand time zones? A bad one.

I made another trip to Boston around Christmastime and was joined by Sy Johnson, the lone mixed signal applications engineer from San Jose and Cindy Kadiz, the HR lady who hired me into SOS. We didn't see much of Sy, he tried to keep West Coast hours so he didn't suffer from jet lag, but I saw Cindy around the office quite a bit. She was an older single woman, very friendly and we enjoyed each other's company going to lunch and dinner while I tried to show her around the area near Burlington. It was her first visit to the Burlington office and she was here to integrate the Axmi people into the new Steppenwolf conglomeration of SOS, Axmi and Sicas. We were all invited to the Axmi Christmas party which was a very elegant affair, some of the attendees even wore tuxedos. Cindy, knowing hardly anyone from Burlington stuck close to me and talked me into dancing with her to the live band. I felt kind of strange dancing with this older woman, but I came up with a solution. I persuaded Sy Johnson to dance with her, and by the end of the evening Sy and Cindy were a couple. The day after the party we all flew back to San Jose and arrived Saturday around 2PM. April and I barely had time to say hello to each other before we had to get on a bus headed for Monterey, California for the Steppenwolf West Coast Christmas party.

Steppenwolf rented the entire Monterey Bay Aquarium for the Christmas party. Remember the "Cetacean Institute" in the movie *Star Trek IV: The Voyage Home*? One in the same. The venue was fantastic, great food, including sushi which seemed rather cruel to the fish swimming in the tanks nearby. The problem was that since April and I had been apart so long, and as I said, had hardly any time to even say hello, we could hardly keep our hands off each other. We kept getting caught smooching at various places in the aquarium and were the talk of the party. Sy and Cindy were together too, which was really nice to see. A few months later Sy and Cindy were married. They made a good couple and I was proud to have been the one that paired them up at the Boston Christmas party.

Steppenwolf closed the Burlington office which the Axmi division had outgrown and moved it to Billerica. It was a bit nicer and by then we were using good hotels again with real restaurants in them so I didn't have to eat hash browns flavored with roofing tar. The people were still the same: assholes, but there were exceptions.

By this time, Will Charlatan and I were friendly and I would occasionally run into him on the road, like one time we stayed at the same hotel in Rancho Bernardo servicing Southern Morse. We spent an evening in the hotel hot tub drinking beer and sharing stories of our exploits. Malcolm Reynolds, the guy who had tested my IQ with the button hole puzzle took a shine to me after I showed him a piece of code I wrote to “unscramble” a waveform to show a single cycle of a wave. Malcolm had done the same thing, but my code was much more efficient than his, so now I had his respect.

One night Will took me out to see a show at the local strip club in Billerica. It was a one-night-only appearance of the world’s fattest stripper. What a horrific sight! She was very rude too. Her show was just so off-putting I never wanted to see anything like that again.

For those who object to businessmen visiting strip clubs, let me just say that if you fail to take customers to strip clubs, you **will** lose the business you seek. When I worked at HiQ in Oregon an engineer from HiQ Malaysia visited for an entire month. Several of us befriended him and took him to lunch and dinner all over the Portland area. On his last night the in U.S. we took him to a strip club. Instead of being grateful he was furious! “Why take me to a strip club on my last day! Why didn’t you take me to this place on my first day?” Clearly he would have liked to visit more of them while in the area and now he wouldn’t get the chance. In another similar incident, we entertained a couple of guys from England while trying to persuade them to buy our testers. We took them to a few strip clubs in the Portland area after carefully broaching the subject (not everyone is game). After their visit, they flew to Minnesota to visit our competition. After a few months we heard that **we** won the business for $1.5 million. The guys we entertained signed up for training and came back to the States. Their first destination after getting off the plane from London was not their hotel, nor was it our facility. Nope, the first place they visited was one of the strip clubs we had taken them to. They spent their days attending training and their nights at the strip clubs. Our competitors did not take them to strip clubs, we did, so we got the business and they didn’t.

One time my boss, Charlene, caught on to the fact that I was arranging a customer outing to the “Oregon Ballet” as it was euphemistically called. She pulled me aside and said, “Dan, why not take these guys to a night club where they can dance with **real** women?” I told her, “Charlene, these guys are all married! They don't want to dance with women, they want to see them naked!" You can be a prude, you can be an upright citizen, you can be a feminist, but you'll be out of work, broke and living on government handouts. Give the customers what they want (within reason of course) and you'll be successful.

Boston had many high quality strip clubs. The biggest and best was the Golden Banana, "The one place you can't take your Nana," as put by a parody of *Copacabana* by Barry Manilow performed by a local Boston radio DJ. One day I was teaching a class and some of the students decided they wanted to go to the Golden Banana up on Route 1 and I decided to join them. I had been there before with a couple of Indian guys, so I knew the way. A fellow Steppenwolf engineer from San Jose, Gary Hawker, was in the class and wanted to join us. Gary is a great guy, fun, brilliant, easy going, just a pleasure to be around. His parents lived in Connecticut and he was staying with them since he seldom made it to the East Coast. At the end of the instructional day we all drove up Route 1 and went into the world famous Golden Banana.

Gary kept reminding everyone that he could only stay for an hour as it was a long drive to his parents' home in Connecticut, but he stayed and stayed and stayed. He got drunker and drunker and drunker. Eventually, at 9PM he left. I had to give him directions because getting southbound wasn't straightforward. Recently the state road crew had put Jersey Barriers in the center of Route 1, so you couldn't just pull out of the parking lot and head south. You had to drive north to the next exit, go over the overpass and then get back on Route 1 southbound and pass by the strip club across the street from the Golden Banana, Casablanca.

The next day we started class without Gary, he was late. By noon we were worried, but finally he called the office and got in touch with me. Leaving the Golden Banana, he had gotten back on Route 1 going south but stopped for one more beer at Casablanca. He closed down Casablanca at 2AM and then drove all the way to Connecticut and made it to his parents' home by 5AM. When his alarm went off at 7AM he was not capable of getting up so he just took the day off.

There was more to do in Boston than going to strip clubs. I went downtown several times and really enjoyed seeing all the sights. It was a vibrant and exciting town. I walked into Cheers, the same one fictionalized on the TV show of the same name. Very disappointing. Small place, low ceilings. Remember that on the TV show it was a walk down place, that explained the low ceilings. I drove to Salem, site of the famous witch trials.

Two guys had gotten into a fender-bender on the road going through town, so they both got out of their cars and got into a fistfight in the middle of the street while everyone stuck in traffic behind them got out of their cars to cheer them on. Lovely people, did I mention that? I drove out to Cape Cod, yeah, it was OK, but Santa Cruz is much nicer, and no snow!

On one trip I was with George McFly trying to sell TestEz testers to LogAnaChip in Cambridge, right across the street from MIT. The night before our meeting with LogAna, we went downtown with a contracting salesman Howard to celebrate St. Patty's Day. Boston was **the** place to be on St. Patty's Day night. All the bars were packed and most had long lines outside to get in. We finally found a place we could get into and got a table upstairs overlooking the main bar. Near our table was a really cute pair of blonde haired, blue eyed identical twins and Howard, who was twice their age was having fun flirting with them. They were from Kansas and were just visiting to see what Boston was like on St. Patty's Day. After a couple of rounds we noticed three U.S. Navy sailors come in the front door of the bar looking for a place to sit down. All three of us, George, Howard and myself had been in the Navy, so we yelled down to the sailors and told them to join us for a couple of free pitchers of beer up on the second floor. They joined us and then Howard really went to work on the twins. He finally persuaded them to join us and have a drink with all six of us. So now it was three lecherous old men and three young sailors and two hot young identical twins. We ordered and paid for two more pitchers of beer and then left the five of them to drink the beer down and work out the logistics of who was going to end up with whom. It was the nicest thing I ever did for a fellow sailor.

The next day George and I had an appointment with Mal Robeson, head of LogAnaChip's Test Engineering department for MEMS products. MEMS stands for Micro-Electro-Mechanical System. Common MEMS products are electronic accelerometers and gyroscopes used for sensing the position and movements of your phone, your car, your tablet, your toy helicopter, your drone, etcetera. We had no experience with MEMS but George found what looked like a good match for the capabilities of the TestEz tester. George did most of the talking and said to Mal, "We are new to mixed signal and we're not sure we know what we are doing." Oh, gee George, thanks a lot! So I started the demonstration on my laptop as Mal watched rather intently. When I was done, Mal turned to George and said, "I think you know what you are doing!" Thank God, and no thanks to George!

Mal enjoyed the demo enough that he gave me a two axis accelerometer to test. I took it back home with me, wired up a socket and in two days had the test program working four times faster than the solution he was using in Boston. Mal was very excited about this result, so he started pushing to get our tester qualified at LogAnaChip. However, his management pushed back, they didn't want a new tester on their test floor, and their reason was rather strange.

LogAnaChip built their own testers, had for years. They also sold them to other competitors, and sometimes they would buy out a competitor and find a whole bank of their own testers on the competitor's test floor. LogAna's tester division was arming the enemy! So they stopped selling their own testers outside the company, but that caused the tester division to become unprofitable, so they had to keep it alive by restricting new, outside testers from getting in the door. We were kept out to keep their own tester division profitable.

Mal was not happy with this decision. Not happy at all. A few months later I got a call from Mal. He wanted George and I to be the first to hear the news: he found a job at a competitor, National Diode and gave his notice at LogAna. I asked him, "Why tell me?" Because, he said, "When I get to my new company, I'm going to buy a bunch of your testers!"

A few month's later we arranged for Red Stevens to visit Nat Diode, but the guys there didn't share Mal's enthusiasm for our tester and all our sales efforts fell flat. I felt bad for Mal, having thrown away a career at a high profile company only to have the same thing happen to him at Nat Diode. Furthermore, National Diode was based in Los Angeles, so guess what? He had to become a Road Warrior too, traveling to LA every week until he got an office opened up in Boston.

I had one more trip to Boston after that, for an interview for Altex just days before Christmas. I decided that I needed to make some more money after retiring to make some modifications to our houseboat, and Altex flew me out there for an interview. I was confident but I hadn't worked in four years and thought I might not be as sharp as I had been in the past. The interview was difficult for me and I started thinking I had blown it. The guys interviewing me were just as mean, if not meaner than the Axmi guys on my first trip out to Boston. They challenged me on my programming abilities, they denied that my patented invention was really a unique invention, and so on. If I got hired, these guys would be my coworkers and I got the feeling that if I asked a question of them they would laugh in my face or just ignore me, the way the Axmi guys had.

Especially damaging was the fact that in the hotel room the night before the interview I realized that my web page had a damning statement about one of Altex's employees, a trainer who was so bad that I dropped out of the class. I was able to log into the FTP server and delete that one line but it was too late. The manager had seen that part of my web page and confronted me about it. I felt like crap, but I admitted that I had already purged the defamatory remark. That sort of fixed it, but by the time I met with the Human Resources person I decided that the whole interview had not gone well and had given up. The HR lady was really sweet and said that she had never seen the manager so excited about a candidate. Of course her remarks were referring to his attitude before the interview. Still, there might be hope.

He walked me out and we said our goodbyes. I felt like crap but went back to the hotel and prepared to go home in defeat. I got up really early so I could get to Logan airport and make my flight. After grabbing a quick breakfast at the hotel breakfast buffet, I got on the road and got confused and all turned around, but finally made it to the airport. I boarded the plane, we taxied out and then the pilot came on the intercom to tell us we were heading back to the gate. There was a small malfunction that they needed to check on. Once at the gate we were told we could leave our carry-ons in the overhead bins if we wanted, but don't go too far because they might call us back to re-board the plane very soon.

Several hours later it became obvious that our plane was not going anywhere. We had to get in line to get back on the plane to get our carry on items. This trip was not going well! Then we all had to get into one of many lines to help us get alternate flights out of Boston. Again, this was just days before Christmas and just like the movie *Planes, Trains and Automobiles*, all the flights were full and it might be nigh impossible to get a plane out. Each person in line ahead of me took up to a half hour of the ticket agent's time, so being tenth in line meant it could be five hours of standing in line.

Finally I got to the front of the line and after about a half hour they were able to get me a flight to Philadelphia in First Class that night, but I had to spend the night in Philly and catch another plane to Phoenix, also First Class, and then another flight in Coach to Portland. They told me to get a hotel voucher once I landed in Philly from one of the gate agents there.

I waited for four hours to get my flight to Philly. When I arrived I had to stand in line again for two more hours to get a hotel voucher so I didn't have to spend the night at the airport. I caught a shuttle to the hotel, got some sleep as I was completely exhausted, both physically and emotionally. The next day I got up and found that the hotel was being remodeled and the restaurant was closed, so no breakfast. I took the shuttle back to the airport and found a Chik-fil-A open in the gate area. There had recently been a big brouhaha over some anti gay remarks by the owner of Chik-fil-A and I was there to do my part in supporting them. A chicken sandwich for breakfast was the best I could do.

I got on the flight and had a comfortable ride in First Class all the way to Phoenix on US Scare. At Phoenix I found a Burger King and filled up on my favorite, then made it to the gate to board the plane to Portland. We got on board but the flight attendant said, "This plane's not going anywhere, they haven't loaded the food and beverage carts." *Now what?* A few minutes later they asked us to disembark, there was a malfunction. Here we go again! Two cancelled flights on the same damn trip! Not only that, I failed the interview! I made a call to a friend in the Phoenix area, Vince Foster, to see if I could stay the night with him, but all I got was his answering machine, so again, I was stuck.

A few hours later they found us a plane that could get us to Portland, but our plans had been completely screwed up. My wife was getting off work at midnight and my flight was supposed to land right about that time so she could come pick me up at the airport. Now my flight was delayed so much that I would not land until 5AM. So after getting off work, my wife tried to sleep, but couldn't so she just stayed up and met me at the airport when I landed at 5AM. We were both beat and emotionally drained. This job with Altex was going to involve more travel and it seemed like it was going to be like this for the rest of my life. Good God, what was I going to do?

A few weeks later I got a call from Altex, congratulating me for getting the job. Oh, Christ I thought! How do I get out of this! My wife had just gotten the job of her dreams (or so she thought) in Vancouver, Washington and this Altex position was in San Jose. I had a big decision to make. A few days later I turned down the offer, $100,000 a year, whereas my wife's job was only going to bring in $20,000 a year, but at least it was in Vancouver, so we wouldn't have to move. Luckily a little later I was able to get an offer from TerroDacNix which got me sent to Dallas, Texas for three weeks, but at least most of the rest of the job was strictly in Beaverton, Oregon. At least I wouldn't be on the road full time like I would have been with the Altex job. Speaking of Texas....

Texas

"Now we see that the TPP Status register is set to 10101100 and because the ADSC Datalog register is set to 11000010 what state are we in?"
"Texas!"
RotoMolded technician's response to my query about the state of the tester during a RadChek RC16 programming class

I've been going to Texas since 1986. My first trip was to Austin, but I also worked in Dallas, Houston and Seguin, just outside of San Antonio, but let's start with my first trip to RotoMolded Oak Hills in Austin.

Oak Hills was the site of RotoMolded's digital fab and test facility where the MC6800 and MC68000 microprocessors were produced. RotoMolded bought a large number of RadChek RC16s to test the 68000 processor that was being used in many applications including the new Apple Macintosh. I was sent there to give the maintenance course where I taught RotoMolded technicians how to take care of the systems, just like I had in Kokomo. These test systems needed lots of TLC; filters needed to be cleaned, power supplies needed periodic adjustments and of course circuit boards would fail and it wasn't necessarily obvious which board was bad. So I had to go to RotoMolded and teach them how to do it all.

Oak Hills was a great facility. The first thing that caught my eye was the speed limit signs in the parking lot. 12MPH, 7MPH or 3MPH. What was that about? When I finally got a chance to ask I was told that it was based on a study that showed that people mostly ignored the typical 10MPH or 5MPH speed limit signs, but when told that the speed limit was 12MPH they would constantly glance at the speedometer to keep the speed at 12 miles per hour as though they assumed there was some special reason for this out of the ordinary speed limit. Once I arrived at the front door I was a little intimidated because they had armed guards in the lobby to keep out dangerous people. I asked why and was told that not long ago the ex-husband of some employee came in with a gun and shot the place up. Once I was cleared through security and inside the building I was free to roam wherever I pleased and I was very impressed. To begin with, RotoMolded had motivational posters everywhere that promoted sensible advice. For example, if you had to make a trip to the restroom and you could carry some mail to the mail room, or you could deliver a box to its destination, you should do that too. In other words, don't waste RotoMolded's time, make good use of the time you are paid for. This was the opposite of what they did at Gizmotronics in Kokomo. However, that doesn't mean that RotoMolded was stingy with work time.

One very interesting program they had was a van-pooling deal that used regular employees as drivers. Drivers/employees were compensated for the extra hours it took them to drive all these employees around so that a vanpool driver only had to work 4 days a week but was paid for a 40 hour week. RotoMolded wasn't stingy, they were just very, very efficient. The employees were very happy people because they were well paid, RotoMolded stock was doing well and the working conditions were very high class. For example, the main cafeteria at the Oak Hills campus was really fantastic. The food choices were great and the dining area featured a huge glass wall that looked out on a scrub oak forest behind the building. RotoMolded built a deer feeding station and kept it filled with food for the deer that lived in the area. During lunch or a break you could sit almost anywhere in the dining room and watch the deer wander in and have a meal. Just amazing!

In contrast to the excellent operations at RotoMolded was the rental car company I was using. I got a phone call at my hotel from them, my rental car's license plate had expired and they wanted me to come back in to the airport office and get a new car with a legitimate license plate. I couldn't believe it! They knew that I was renting this car for three weeks, so why give me **that** car? Idiots! I drove back to the airport and exchanged cars after giving the manager a piece of my mind. They didn't bother me after that.

Back at RotoMolded, we had a very modern classroom with white boards, overhead projector, new furniture, and coffee and snacks delivered regularly. That was a really great perk, especially for a coffee junkie like me. However, the majority of our work had to be done on the Test Floor where millions upon millions of chips were tested. We didn't have to wear bunny suits but we did have to "smock up" so that we didn't pollute the environment and create static problems. I would put "bugs" in the systems that we were assigned to use and let the students try to find them using the skills I taught them in the classroom. I also assigned them to perform preventive maintenance which they could do alone once I showed them the basics. So while the students changed air filters, or adjusted power supplies or made other adjustments I had time on my hands, but I still had to stay close by in case they came up with a question or other issue. I took up a position on the test floor and just stood there waiting for someone to pester me.

Word got out that *The RadChek Guy* was on site, so people who weren't even in the class would come up and ask me questions. I was thrilled! I was suddenly the onsite expert for the RC16 and many people, both technicians and engineers sought me out to ask questions that had bothered them but had not yet been answered by their local applications engineer. I was the most knowledgable person around and it was a great feeling.

My main interface was a guy named Henry Winkler. Henry was a technician who learned enough about programming to become a very valuable asset to RotoMolded in the realm of test engineering. The problem for Henry was that RotoMolded required a Bachelor's of Science degree in Electrical Engineering (BSEE) to be a test engineer. When an opening in test engineering appeared on the bulletin board, Henry applied and was turned down. It was such a shame because he was a really sharp guy. Henry decided he wasn't going to stand for that crap, so he went over to MAD, also in Austin and got an offer for a job as a test engineer. When Henry gave his two week notice, RotoMolded freaked out and offered him an equivalent position at RotoMolded, ignoring their requirement for a BSEE. Henry was pleased, so he stayed and kept his seniority. Again, a true sign of a top notch corporation.

Austin seemed to be a decent place, and I did enjoy my stay at the Wyndham Hotel down the road from Oak Hills. By now I fully understood how I should structure my expense report to avoid trouble, so I was able to live well. I drove a new car, ate at great places, made sure to include most of my beverages in with the meal so that I didn't have to buy too much beer on my own dime. In addition I knew people in the area.

Buck Fry, who had previously worked in Tech Support at RadChek in San Jose, moved to Austin to support RotoMolded and MAD. He invited me to his home, which he bragged had cost him one quarter what the same house in San Jose would cost. It was tempting to consider a transfer like that! Buck had a problem though: Buck's drug connection was in San Jose, and he could not get marijuana in Texas. So his friend, Whitey Folger who worked in Software Support, would send Buck an occasional software update in a 5MB Phoenix disk pack with an extra baggie in the box. Sometime later Whitey ended up in the local prison for a very serious DUI hit and run accident.

I made several trips to Oak Hills to teach classes, but once I was asked to create a special class for the technicians. The idea was that I would teach the technicians how to read an MC68000 test program and show them how to use IDP, the Interactive Debug Program, so that when a test program failed to work properly, but the diagnostics didn't report a failure (which happened occasionally), the technicians might have a chance of figuring out the real problem by running the debugger. RotoMolded sent me the program that I should use and I spent several weeks developing a one week class and then flew down to Austin to teach it.

I always found the RotoMolded technicians to be very intelligent, so I didn't hold back on details. Day after day I would walk them through the code and then let them single step through the program line by line in the afternoon on the test floor to get the feel for it. During one session we were deep in the code trying to keep track of all the register states so we all knew what was going on. At one point I decided it would be a good idea to make sure everyone was keeping up so I said to the class, "OK, what state are we in?" This one big Texan picked up his feet, slammed his garishly bejeweled cowboy boots on the table in front of him and proudly exclaimed, "Texas!" I was so impressed with the national pride of the Texans, and this guy epitomized Texans and the pride they feel in their state.

Then on the last day of the class I was told that the technicians were not going to be provided a copy of the latest version of the program. There was no way to troubleshoot a problem in the debugger without a current program listing, so the whole week had been a waste of time, not to mention the weeks of course development time. Too bad to say the least!

In my off time I found fun things to do in the area. On one trip a guy from RotoMolded Indonesia was enrolled in the class, and while all the other students lived in the Austin area, this poor guy was spending his weekends alone in his hotel room. So one weekend, I decided to hang out with him and see if we could have some fun. It was a super hot weekend, so I suggested that we drive out to Lake Travis, named for the hero from the Alamo, to keep cool. I let him drive which was a huge mistake. On the freeway he would floor the accelerator until his speed was in the upper seventies then he would slam on the brakes and get the speed back down to fifty-five again. Then mash the gas again, up to almost eighty. We made it out to Lake Travis and found a clean, sandy beach near the dam. We spent the whole day, neck deep in the cool water, drinking beer. No need to get out, just stay cool and keep drinking. Sort of the same way kids swimming in Walden Pond did it.

On another trip to Austin I decided to drive down to San Antonio to check out the Alamo and the Riverwalk. I was really impressed with the Riverwalk, which is featured in several movies including *Cloak and Dagger* with Dagney Coleman. A few years later when I was at Steppenwolf, the guys in Billerica Massachusetts had built a special tester for RotoMolded, who was building engine control modules for Floored. I flew out to Boston, learned the tester and then flew to San Antonio with three coworkers who had never been to Texas. We were going to be working in Seguin, Texas which was about 45 miles east of San Antonio. Seguin was a tiny town with only one hotel and glimmers of Kokomo flooded back, so I convinced the other guys on my team to stay with me at the Holiday Inn right on the Riverwalk in San Antonio. That way we could get up in the morning and drive to Seguin to do our work there, then drive back to San Antonio and party all night on the Riverwalk. Boy, did we have fun! We hit a place named *Dicks Last Stand* on the Riverwalk. Dicks served food and drink with an attitude. The waitresses were told to be flippant and cruel to the patrons and we were welcome to treat them the same way. There was a chubby Mexican waitress wearing a white T-shirt with the words "Kiss me where I pee" scrawled in permanent marker across the chest. We were lucky, our waitress treated us well and we enjoyed a wonderful meal, then we walked further down the Riverwalk to drink some more. One morning I was certain that I would be going to Seguin alone because the other two Steppenwolf guys were too hung over. Finally they got up and came with me to the plant.

The RotoMolded plant in Seguin was very impressive, much like the one in Oak Hills in Austin, but it was laid out much differently because it had a singular purpose. The plant had a single assembly line that started with a bare circuit board on one end and put out a fully assembled and tested Floored engine control module for either 4, 6 or 8 cylinder Floored cars and trucks at the other end. In the last station our tester checked them over fully before they were boxed up and sent to Floored. Again, RotoMolded really had it together like every other facility.

One feature of the building was the main restrooms off the manufacturing floor. There were two doors, one for men and one for women, but the door into the restroom was a one-way door, you were not allowed to exit the door you came into, and there was no handle on the inside of the door. You were to use the restroom, which had no sinks inside, and then leave out the exit! The exits at the end of both the men's and women's bathroom put you into a common hand washing area between the two restrooms with nothing but sinks. That way, when you came out of the restroom, if you failed to wash your hands, people of both sexes could see you walk past the two walls lined with sinks and everyone on the manufacturing floor would see you, too. They used shame to induce everyone to wash their hands, and boy, did it work! It virtually never happened and if it did, some supervisor or manager would catch the miscreant and shame them into compliance. That is one reason I always respected RotoMolded.

RotoMolded had another test facility in Austin, called Ed Bluestein. What Oak Hills was to digital products, Ed Bluestein was to analog and mixed signal. I was asked to give an SOS3000 mixed signal class at Ed Bluestein and again, for the most part enjoyed my time in Austin. The engineers were really smart, but some of them complained that RotoMolded ran random drug tests so that they could not smoke marijuana on the weekends. I was sympathetic to their plight, especially because their boss would pick me up at the lobby every morning reeking of alcohol. Was he drinking in the morning? It could be, which made the drug tests rather ridiculous, but being RotoMolded, that's just the way they did things.

I also made several trips to Dallas, which I had flown through several times but never got out of the airport to have a look around. On one trip I flew into Austin, visited some customers with the sales guy, Joe Campanella and the applications manager, Vince Foster. We rented a car which was designated as nonsmoking even though Joe smoked, and drove to Dallas to visit some customers there. Joe was having a really hard time with the no-smoking restriction in this nonsmoking rental car so our journey to Dallas was punctuated by several stops to let Joe have a smoke. I had given up smoking years ago and so was rather annoyed with his addictive behavior. While we were driving up to Dallas we were stopped in our tracks by a very violent thunderstorm. We pulled into a truck stop and waited it out while Joe puffed away furiously, savoring his freedom. In Kokomo storms like this often resulted in tornados. I sure as heck didn't want to die in a tornado at a truck stop in Texas!

Once in Dallas, we stopped by several customers and one visit had a humorous start. We got to an unmanned lobby and Joe put in a call to the customer to come let us into the building. While waiting Joe decided to try out a blood pressure monitor built on to a small desk. So Joe sat down, put his arm into the blood pressure cuff and pushed the button. The cuff inflated automatically and then started deflating slowly to measure his blood pressure. The customer appeared at the door to let us in and there is Joe, trapped in the cuff. He stands up, his arm now securely attached to the desk and he can't get free until the monitor finishes measuring his blood pressure. We all enjoyed a good laugh at Joe's expense.

Once all our customer visits were complete, we drove to the airport so Vince and I could fly out of Dallas and then Joe would drive the rental car back to Austin. As we waived goodbye, Joe lit up a cigarette, climbed into the nonsmoking rental car and drove away. Good luck getting your rental car deposit back Vince!

A year later, Joe asked me to create a special training course for Arlen ChipPhab that would cover the analog only on the TestEz, but would not cover any of the mixed signal instruments. ChipPhab apparently didn't buy the mixed signal instruments and didn't want the class to cover them, fearing that I would turn into a high pressure sales opportunity. That required some intricate surgery on the course because the mixed signal and analog were so tightly intertwined. I went to Arlen ChipPhab and picked up Joe who flew in from Austin. Apparently Joe set the customer's expectations a bit differently than I had expected. So now, I'm teaching the class to gaggle of engineers who expected to learn the Digital Signal Processing (DSP) statements as well as the analog. I had chopped out much of the DSP information from the course because the analog instruments don't require DSP. The DSP statements are most useful in concert with the mixed signal instruments, but it is almost impossible to disentangle the two because there is no way to teach the DSP functions without also talking about the mixed signal instruments, which they did not own and did not want to hear about. It's like having to teach someone how to change a tire on a car, but with the stipulation that you don't say a word about the actual car. It's hard to talk about jacking up the car to change the tire if you aren't allowed to talk about the car. They complained about the class after I went home and I was forced to defend myself in front of a group of sales guys who could not understand what the problem was. I never went back to Arlen ChipPhab which was good, and bad, in some ways.

A bit later Joe called and asked me to come visit a new potential customer in Dallas, a few hours visit for two days of travel. OK, fine. I got up at 4AM and drove my van to the airport. On the way there my transmission started groaning and grinding and I knew I was in trouble. I kept driving and ground, screeched and rattled my way into the long term parking lot at PDX. Once I checked into my flight I called my wife and told her what had happened and asked if she could do something about it. It took her hours to convince the parking lot people to let her and the AAA tow truck driver get to the van. We had towing coverage, but not enough to get it towed all the way back to Beaverton where our normal shop was. The tow truck driver told her that for an additional $25 we could get unlimited towing coverage and it would apply to this tow. That decision was easy, unlike the rest of the ordeal. In the meantime I made it to Dallas, Joe picked me up and told me that this whole trip was probably a waste of time, but it gave him something to do. I was so mad at him I could have spit. After all my wife had been through I should have punched him in the face, but I kept my cool and did the visit. I spent the night in an Embassy Suites that had seen better days. My room had the scorched imprint of the an iron burned into the carpet. Apparently someone plugged in the iron, turned it on and just left it on the carpet.

After I joined TerroDacNix, I had to make a three week trip to Raygunz in Dallas, just two days after my start date. Raygunz was part of the Instruments of Texas campus, the building and the employees had been bought from IOT by Raygunz after IOT decided to get out of the military electronics business. TerroDacNix was now taking over the test portion of this business, although Raygunz kept control of the manufacturing. This was supposed to save Raygunz money. They might have done like many other manufacturers and moved the testing to Asia, but since these were military products they were not eligible for transfer outside the U.S.

I made the trip with two coworkers, Walt Cronkite and Jose Sanchez, an immigrant from Peru. They got a rental car and I got a rental car, which was great because we were going to be there for a long time and while they seemed like good guys, I like having a little independence.

During my interview at TerroDacNix I was asked by one of the senior managers how I was at handling difficult customers. I had encountered many difficult customers in the past and told him about a few of them. One was a customer in Taiwan who was very unhappy with the new million dollar testers he bought. The customer insisted that he be allowed to dictate to me an email that I was to send to the Steppenwolf CEO, Heath Kitt at the time. I wrote down everything he said and then emailed it to the CEO. I courtesy copied the customer on the email and this satisfied him completely. My story choice was advantageous because the difficult customer he was talking about was an Asian gal named Xiaoling, but their nickname for her was The Dragonlady. Xiaoling was a very tough customer according to everyone at TerroDacNix. Walt admitted that the last time he was in Dallas, he nearly became an alcoholic trying to recover from his daily run-ins with Xiaoling. It would be a challenge, but I was there to do my best.

We all three got suites in a hotel very near the Raygunz plant and I rode along to work with the other guys since they knew the way. We met with the crew that we would be replacing. The guys who were training us were going to lose their jobs once we were up to speed, and that made for a few tense moments during our stay. Overall they were very friendly and competent guys, it was Xiaoling who was to be feared.

The most visible Raygunz test engineer, the most respected engineer there was Mark Spitz. He didn't swim, but he did sport the same fancy name as the world famous athlete. Every Thursday he had to take off work to get this special cancer treatment that had been flown in to DFW airport the previous day. Apparently it had a very short shelf life so it was crucial that Mark take half a day off every Thursday. Since we had limited time, only three weeks, this caused us many scheduling problems, but we got through that.

The Raygunz campus was fairly modern and opulent, and there were some impressive things going on there. Not only did they build and test military hardware, but space hardware too. This was right up Xiaoling's alley. Once while I was waiting in our temporary office for tester time, Xiaoling visited me and we chatted casually. She told me that she used to work for NASA and once sat in the pilot's seat of a Space Shuttle on the launch pad. I was impressed! She didn't sound like a scary person.

We would start every morning with a one to two hour meeting with Xiaoling to set the goals of the day and figure out priorities so that we didn't waste time. On the second day I watched Walt and Xiaoling get into it. Walt was being rather boneheaded in my humble opinion, and Xiaoling took charge and got nasty with him. It looked more like this was just an ongoing pissing contest between Walt and Xiaoling because otherwise she was a super sweet lady. On March 14, Pi day (3/14) she brought in a dozen cupcakes, pointing out that cupcakes were easier to share during our morning meeting than having to cut up slices of pie. Very cute I thought.

I did have one run in with Xiaoling on this trip, but it wasn't really very confrontational. One of the test boxes, a computer controlled Arbitrary Waveform Generator (AWG) quit working. Raygunz didn't have a backup AWG and so in the morning meeting we were discussing what to do about it. I suggested that to make sure we meet the deadline, I just go out and rent one. Xiaoling scoffed at me saying, "Oh Dan, you are so naive!" A bit taken aback I explained that I owned a credit card and even if the company didn't reimburse me that would be OK, I could live with that. I then told the story that I had heard in a Tom Peters' motivational lecture on employee empowerment. A FedEx supervisor hired a helicopter to take him to a telephone relay tower that the phone company refused to fix because it was being buried in a snow storm. FedEx customer service relied on that phone line for package tracking requests. The supervisor was flown up to the phone company's relay tower, fixed it and saved the day for FedEx, which more than made up for a low level supervisor renting a helicopter. Any normal company would have fired him, instead FedEx gave him a bonus.

We figured out a way to work around the problem without having to rent a helicopter, but because this incident didn't become toxic, Xiaoling and I continued to have cordial relations throughout my trip.

So every day the three of us TerroDacNix folks, me, Walt and Jose would get up in the morning, meet for breakfast at the hotel's free breakfast buffet, discuss our plans for the day, drive to Raygunz, meet with Xiaoling and the crew in the morning and get to work on the test floor by 10AM. Then at lunchtime we would meet in the Raygunz cafeteria with the guys whose jobs we were stealing and try to downplay the evilness of our role there.

I had been hired so quickly that TerroDacNix didn't have a chance to get me a company credit card. Walt, being my supervisor told me that I should not spend my own money on meals because it was harder to justify on the expense reports, so he would pay for all the meals and expense them himself. At the Raygunz cafeteria I would select my lunch for a vast array of gastronomic delights and then wait at the cashier's register telling her that I was waiting for my "wife" to pay. Washington state had just legalized same-sex marriage, so it was kind of a fun joke, but Walt was not pleased with my insinuating that we were a gay couple. Still, it was hard to resist, especially in Texas where that kind of thing is very much looked down on.

At the end of the day, around 6PM, we would be exhausted, but the day was not over. We would drive back to the hotel and then meet with the TerroDacNix sales guy, Ford Littlejohn by phone. We spent about a half hour doing that, then we would go out to dinner. We would get back to the hotel around 9PM and have the rest of our night to ourselves. My normal bed time was 9:30PM so I didn't get much free time. I planned on doing some consulting work for another company while in Dallas, but I just couldn't do it! There wasn't enough time in the day and I got nowhere, so I just had to drop that job which would have paid me $10,000 if I could have completed it.

One thing I found that was kind of strange is that Walt and Jose both did their own laundry in the laundry room at the hotel. I asked why they didn't just let the hotel do it, like I had always done everywhere else I had been. Walt explained that he didn't think the company would cover the high cost of having the hotel get it sent out, but being new to the company I had checked the travel policy and it was clearly allowed. After that I just ignored Walt's admonishments and let the hotel handle my laundry. Meanwhile, Walt and Jose ran up the meal expenses as high as was allowed, so while they might have saved money on laundry, they sure as hell didn't seem to care about spending on meals.

Our first weekend there, we got behind enough that Walt and I had to go in and work on Saturday. Jose flew his girlfriend in so they spent the weekend together in Dallas while Walt, Xiaoling and I spent most of Saturday at Raygunz working to catch up.

The next weekend I was free, so I drove my rental car out to Bullard, Texas, about 2 hours east of Dallas, just south of Tyler. The name Bullard was everywhere, but it seemed I was the only Bullard in town. I thought this would make me a celebrity but despite being a Saturday I could not find anyone in town to talk to, let alone brag about being a Bullard in Bullard, Texas. I took a hundred or so photos and then headed back to Dallas.

The last week got intense. We were still a bit behind and I made some blunders that put me even more behind. I had to retake several hours worth of data on one of the devices and didn't get to finish. My flight left for home Friday night while Walt and Jose were staying till next Tuesday. Because he was going to be there over the weekend anyway Walt took over for me and let me make my flight. I was rather shocked when I got to DFW around 6PM to see nearly all the restaurants closing up before I could get some dinner. I was really starting to worry that I might have to get on the plane to Phoenix without anything to eat but I finally found a bar that served food, so I didn't have to starve all the way to Arizona.

Three weeks away from home is my limit. I know people who do it for months, but I just can't take it! So long Texas, it was fun while it lasted, but I don't think I'll be visiting any time soon!

After I returned to Beaverton, Oregon, Xiaoling and I would develop a friendship that seemed to inspire jealousy in every one of my coworkers. We got along really, really well which was curious because as I mentioned, her name was uttered in fear and loathing at TerroDacNix.

One day I was sitting in a Beaverton conference call meeting with everyone in Dallas on the phone except Xiaoling, who was on vacation that week. It wasn't unusual for Xiaoling to text me during these meetings when she was in Dallas. She would say things like, "Can you believe he said that?" or "That's a load of crap, don't you agree?" (I did). But since she was on vacation I didn't expect to hear from her. How wrong I was.

Xiaoling knew that I would be in this weekly lunchtime meeting starving for lunch as the folks in Dallas droned on and on (they already had *their* lunch). Despite being on vacation, Xiaoling texted me a picture of *her lunch* on my phone, knowing that I was dying for lunch while stuck in this meeting. She planned to torment me! After that we would often send each other pictures of the lunches we were eating, especially when it was Asian cuisine. She was a true American girl but being Asian she loved Asian food, and her Texas underlings would have none of it, especially sushi. I was the only white person she knew who also loved Asian food including sushi, or *bear food* as the Texans called it.

While in Dallas we experienced other cuisines too. I introduced Jose to sushi as well as Pho, Vietnamese beef noodle soup. We found it at a place on Lover's Lane called Pho Is For Lovers. Jose introduced the rest of us to Peruvian cuisine at a place in Dallas that served goat. Not a steak mind you, nor a roast, it was a roasted goat knee. He ordered something else because, as he explained it, the Spanish word goat, cabra is used to insult homosexuals, as in "Hey cabrón, did you get lucky last night with Miguel?" Of course Jose didn't mention that until all of us white guys ordered the goat. *Ah yes, the goat.*

Xiaoling and her crew made a few trips out to Beaverton to make sure we got everything up and running. Xiaoling and I organized after work outings for her guys including two cruises aboard riverboats on the Columbia and Willamette rivers. When Jose asked me why I was doing this, I told him that I thought it was wrong for us to expect them to sit in their hotel rooms while they visited our fair and beautiful Oregon. He retorted that the Raygunz people didn't entertain **us** when we were in Dallas. I couldn't believe it! Since when was the standard for our behavior to be based on their behavior? If we can do better than they did, and it wasn't hard, then why shouldn't we? Jose had been excluded from our outings because Xiaoling didn't like him. When I invited Walt to go aboard the Portland Spirit with the crew, knowing that he would refuse, his fangs came out and the venom started dripping. "I can't think of a worse way to spend my time off than to be stuck on a boat with Xiaoling." See what I mean? The venom in this relationship came not from Xiaoling, she was the sweetest manager I had ever met. No, the whole reason that TerroDacNix feared Xiaoling was Walt's hatred of Xiaoling, for who knows what reason.

Besides, all this goodwill paid off. Instead of balking at traveling to Portland, the Raygunz guys looked forward to their trips. After all the fun we had going on cruises and visiting cool places like Multnomah Falls, Mark Spitz, the Raygunz senior engineer, tried to get TerroDacNix to hire him so he could live in Oregon. Everyone in Dallas had been offered a job and move to Oregon, but they all refused. However, given some time with me being the de-facto goodwill ambassador and tour guide, some of them started reconsidering. Too bad I hadn't been in charge of this deal earlier in the process!

The best thing that came out of my time there was my relationship with Xiaoling. We both cultivated a great friendship that allowed us to turn very difficult and frustrating work days into hours and hours of fun. I would fetch ice water for her while she sat in the conference room-cum-Raygunsz office that I renamed "Xiaoling's Retreat." Despite the government rules that said you can't buy things for vendors, she would order lunch for me, or bring in treats. I would respond by bringing in donuts for her and the crew. I even fetched her Dim Sum for a lunchtime meeting with the Navy guys. While everyone else ate greasy pizza, Xiaoling savored little Chinese dumplings that I hand picked for her. All the other attendees were jealous as hell. Using respect and friendship, not venom, I tamed the "Dragonlady."

After I was laid off from TerroDacNix, my very first layoff ever, Xiaoling championed my return and rehiring, but something happened, I don't know what. Xiaoling sent me a final text telling me what a good engineer I was and that I would find something else. It was the Big Goodbye. My response to my dear friend was classic. Inspired by the movie *Casablanca* I responded, "We'll always have Dallas."

Mr. Misrell: *This is a push business, Williams. A push push push business. Push and drive! .... A push push push business, Williams. It's push push push, all the way, all the time! It's push push push, all the way, all the time, right on down the line!*

The Twilight Zone, A Stop At Willoughby by Rod Serling

Other U.S. ports of call

"This is your captain speaking, just a heads up. The runway at Islip, New York is very short, so as soon as this bird touches down we will be heavy on the brakes. No need to worry though, we've done this many, many times. Have a good flight."

Pilot's address while preparing to land at Islip Long Island, New York.

I will not cover every bloody place I visited in the U.S. There are just way too many places and I doubt that I could recollect all the crazy things that happened to me, but some trips really stand out.

While I was still at RadChek, I was asked to give an onsite training course on programming the RC16 tester at Microtard (now Hauppauge Tardware) in Hauppauge, New York on Long Island. I flew to Chicago and then waited for my flight to Islip, the nearest airport to Hauppauge. Our flight departure was delayed for some reason but finally we boarded the 737 and took off. The pilot warned us it would be a challenging landing because the Islip L.I. airport runway was very, very short compared to most places. He had to put the plane on the runway at the very beginning and then mash the brakes and hope that we stopped before we hit the end of the runway. It was a good thing he warned us because I would have been white knuckled if I hadn't known. As we made our final approach I could see the TV antennas of the single family homes on the approach. I was certain that the residents weren't happy with having planes coming in so low over their homes, but what could be done? Without air service, businesses can't operate.

Once on the ground I had to laugh at the outdoor baggage claim conveyor amid the snow and cold. I got my huge suitcase off the belt and found a place to wait for the Dollar rental car shuttle bus. We arrived a little late because of our delayed departure from Chicago but it was not unusual for flights to be late.

After about an hour of waiting I decided to hail a cab and see if he could take me to the rental office. He told me he knew where it was and drove me there. I was so happy to see the "Open" sign on the door of Dollar Rent-A-Car shack. I wrestled my bulky suitcase out of the trunk, paid the driver and off he went as I went to the door. It was locked.

Goddamn it! That's why the shuttle bus didn't come to get me at the airport. My plane was late and they just went home at 5PM. They knew I was coming in, and it wasn't my fault the plane was late! So now what the hell was I supposed to do? Contrary to popular belief, New York is not a monolithic block of businesses with taxi cabs running up and down the roads.

Here I was at a suburban rent-a-car office buried in a neighborhood with nothing around but a small grocery store. I looked for a phone booth but there weren't any around. I went to the store and asked to use the phone, but the couple running the store didn't even speak English! Am I still in the U.S.?

Well, sort of I guess. I finally made it clear that I needed the phone and the phone book. I called a cab and waited outside with my massive suitcase, packed for two weeks of cold weather. While I waited a gang of hoodlums sauntered by looking me up and down trying to decide whether to roll me. My cab pulled up and I was never so happy to see that scruffy yellow car.

The cabbie took me to the Howard Johnson's in Hauppauge, and charged me a hefty sum for doing it. Oh well, just get a receipt, nothing I can do about this, it wasn't my fault. The next morning at breakfast in the adjoining Howard Johnson's restaurant I heard an interesting exchange between the waitress and a customer. After getting his breakfast he reminded the waitress that he had ordered a **large** orange juice, not a small. She had given him a large, just that a large OJ in New York would be a small, or even a child's portion anywhere else. The waitress flipped out and started yelling at the businessman who had just innocently asked for clarification what constituted a large OJ. Poor guy I thought. Oh, wait. I have to spend two weeks here, poor me!

I took a taxi to Microtard and started teaching the class. They owned two RC16 testers, so that manufacturing could have one and we could have the other. Overall it was a well behaved class, although there were some exceptions. One day I was teaching Match Mode, the same feature that gave the Kokomo engineers including Richard Cadillac so much trouble. One of the students asked me how long it would take the tester to give up if the test didn't pass. Being completely ignorant of the automatic "match mode timeout" feature of Slumburger Sentry testers I told him, "There has to be some intelligence in front of the keyboard because there sure as hell isn't any intelligence behind it." The whole class burst out laughing.

During the first day I was able to get Dollar Rent-A Car on the phone and told the guy there I wanted my rental car delivered. He told me he was the only guy in the office and that was not possible. One of the engineers offered to give me a ride over to the office so I could get my car. I tried not to show my anger at him leaving me stranded at the airport, and then locking office with the Open sign still hanging in the window, but I was not pleased. Finally, I got my car, and of course it gave me flashbacks to my experience I had in Dallas where they rented me a car with an expired license plate. I was crossing off rental car companies one by one. Eventually the only company I would use was Avis, even if the company objected. You want me to travel? You let me use Avis, the only company that hasn't screwed me.

Things went well for most of my time there, but one day we came back from lunch and were not allowed back in the building for a couple of hours. One of the operators, an older woman suffered a heart attack while eating lunch and vomited all over the lunch room. After they cleaned it up we were allowed back in, but the lunch room was off limits for the rest of the day. That was a problem because the engineers spent most of their workday in the lunchroom. Back then computers were slow, and most of the engineers spent their days designing hardware, then running the simulator which took hours to yield results. So the typical day for a Microtard engineer consisted of spending an hour doing design, then sitting in the lunchroom for a couple of hours waiting for the simulator to finish cranking away and toss out a result. If the result showed an error or a fault in the design, a few minutes work would then result in a couple more hours of sitting in the lunch room screwing off. What a way to earn a living!

Of course what I did wasn't that much different. Every diagnostic program we ran to check the hardware took at least a half hour to run, and some took many hours. We would spend hours sitting in chairs in front of the tester watching the screen for failures. I felt a little guilty sometimes, but that was the way things were back then, and there was no alternative.

The weekend came and I decided to drive down to New Jersey to visit my old friends Mike and Cathy. We had been neighbors a few years before in Vallejo, California, but they had since moved back east. To get to New Jersey I had to drive west on Long Island through Hicksville to Brooklyn, within sight of Manhattan. I was very impressed with the skyline of Manhattan so I took an off ramp and drove around downtown New York City. It was impossible to find a place to park so I didn't bother stopping, but it was fun to at least see New York from the street level.

Once I had my fill of New York City I found a freeway onramp and took the Verrazano Narrows bridge to New Jersey by way of the New Jersey Turnpike. Toll after toll, after toll. Oh my God, how did these people live like this! The trick was to get on the Express Lane only if you were going a long distance. If you were in the Express Lane at the wrong place in your journey you were going to be forced to drive several miles, even tens of miles past your off-ramp. I finally made it to Asbury Park where Mike and Cathy lived.

We had a pleasant visit and we even went down the beach on the Atlantic Ocean on Ocean Avenue. The place was a dump. The beach was dotted with garbage cans, but they were full to the point of overflowing and trash blew all up and down the beach. Who the heck would want to go to the beach here? The people who lived there didn't seem to mind.

I said goodbye and was able to make it back through New York and Brooklyn to the hotel without too much trouble. Remember that this was before cell phones and handheld GPS units. I did it all with just a map, which seems amazing now that I think about it.

One day during my second week there I locked my keys in the rental car. I called the rental car company and, again, they were unable to help me. One of the engineers drove me over to the office to get the spare key and I had to promise that I would bring the spare key back at the end of the day. I can't imagine what reason they had for this requirement because it's not like they were keeping it just in case I needed to be rescued from locking my keys in the car! Boy, I really hated this place!

Since the last week of the class happened just before Christmas, I was invited to the company Christmas party to be held onsite the Friday night before my flight back home on Saturday. I accepted and was amazed at what I saw. The CEO was dressed up as Santa Claus and his wife was dressed up as Mrs. Claus. OK, fair enough, but now they called out employees to get their gifts and most of them were very inappropriate for a conservative like me. Female employees were expected to sit on Santa's lap and were given lingerie, sexy panties and even sex toys like vibrators. Male employees were required to sit on Mrs. Claus' lap and get similarly themed gifts. Wow I thought, I'm so glad I don't work here full time, no matter how much sitting around in the cafeteria you're allowed to do.

RadChek started sliding down the tubes as the competing system, the Altex Tritium came out, which they designed and built using people Altex had stolen from RadChek. The demand for training classes fell off steeply and I had less and less to do. However, I did have quite a few customers calling me for help with various problems. Why call the trainer when RadChek still employed a whole department of Tech Support engineers? Because the customers all knew me, I had trained nearly all the customers out there. Furthermore, I was the first employee in the office in the morning and I had recently gotten on this newfangled tool called E-mail. So I was the first person to see customer requests for assistance and I would respond. In most cases I was able to answer all questions a full two hours before the Tech Support crew dragged their sorry asses into work. They saw the number of their calls drop so low that they had nothing to do all day, like Roary Gay who sat in his cubical all day reading the newspaper.

Suddenly I had plenty to do even though there was little demand for training classes. In several cases, the problems needed onsite hands-on assistance, so I asked my boss, Pat Anthony, if I could fly to those sites and help out. Pat agreed and I became a traveling tech support guy. Because I was so good at solving problems I was sent all over, but one of my most memorable trips was back to Hauppauge, New York.

For years, one of the two RC16s at Microtard had a problem that no one was able to solve. Recently, it got so bad that they could not even use the tester. So Adolf, the German engineer I met earlier in Kokomo, the local guy, Dirk McMichaels and I were assigned to go to Hauppauge to see if we could fix the problem.

The problem we were asked to look at was strange. Every so often, with no obvious cause, this one RC16 would get a System Fault which would cause the computer to halt and require a reboot. However, the RC16 right across the aisle ran flawlessly. Dirk had tried to figure it out for years, but never had any luck. So Adolf, Dirk and I began working on the problem sixteen hours a day.

We connected an LED to the SysFault line going back to the Test Controller so we could tell when we got a SysFault signal, then we started swapping things out. We swapped power supplies in the morning, and by evening, the SysFault LED would quiet down completely! Had we solved the problem? Nope, the next morning the SysFault LED would be flashing away wildly. So then we swapped out the whole power controller unit, a 500 pound behemoth. By the time we had it all put back together, the SysFault LED would be quiet. Had we solved the problem? Nope, the next morning it was flashing wildly. We swapped out computers, we swapped out Test Controllers, there is almost nothing in the tester we didn't swap. Every evening the LED would quiet down, and the next morning it would be flashing like crazy. Two weeks of this without a day off was really starting to take its toll, but we kept going, we had no choice. We were told we could not leave until the problem was solved.

Then one day as we were swapping out fans on the top of the tester that kept the circuit boards in the cabinet below cool, something strange happened. The SysFault LED was flashing wildly that morning, but suddenly it stopped! Had we solved the problem? We put the original fan back in, yet the LED did not start flashing again. This was odd! We swap the fan out, and the LED stops flashing, we put the original back in and yet the SysFault LED was still not flashing. Strange. Then I put the fan cover back over the top of the cabinet and the LED started flashing again. The fan cover was a metal box about 2 feet by 2 feet and about 1 foot tall. It had to be removed to get to the fans. I took the fan cover off and the LED quit flashing. I put the fan cover back on, the LED started flashing again! How in the hell could a metal fan cover with no electronic parts cause a SysFault? I looked up at the ceiling and noticed this little gray rubber probe sticking out of a ceiling tile, right above the fan cover that seemed to be causing the problem. "What is that?" I asked.

"Oh, that's an ionizer probe. It keeps the level of static charge down to make sure that we don't have an Electrostatic Discharge issue zapping our chips" the maintenance manager answered. ESD is a big problem in electronic manufacturing environments and causes millions upon millions of dollars of damage annually. Years ago, Microtard bought a system that measured the overall level of static electricity in the air and when it got high, the probes would rain ions charged with the opposite polarity of the charge detected by the controller. I asked if I could remove the probe. The manager said, "Sure, but that's not the problem. The company that makes it told us it would not cause any problems with our equipment."

I removed the probe, no SysFault. I replaced the fan cover. No SysFault. We watched it for hours. No SysFaults. We had seen this before, so we cleaned up the tester and went back to the hotel, expecting to see more SysFaults the next morning. When we arrived the next morning the system was still clean, no SysFaults. That was it! However, we got quite a bit of push-back from the customer. They swore there was no reason that the ionizer would cause this behavior. However, you couldn't argue with success, we solved the problem and explained why they tester across the aisle had never experienced this SysFault error. We checked the ceiling tiles above the other tester, no ionizer probes.

With the problem solved I was allowed to go home and said goodbye to Dirk and Adolf. A few weeks later I got a call from Dirk. The root cause of the problem had been found. A new operator was recently hired and was caught wearing panty hose, contrary to the specific instructions given to test floor personnel. Panty hose worn under the antistatic lab coats generates a ton of static and the ionizer controller noted the increase in static charge, so it would rain ions on the tester and cause SysFaults. The operator worked the day shift and so of course, by day we would get many SysFaults because this gal was on the test floor generating static with her panty hose. At the end of the day when she went home, the static charge went away, the ionizer would stop raining ions on our tester and we were fooled into thinking that we had solved the problem with our day's labor. However, when she showed up the next morning, ions would rain down on the tester and we would be right back where we started. It was all their fault, the tester was not at fault in any way. I wonder what RadChek charged the customer for three top engineers slaving away sixteen hours a day for almost three weeks?

After that trip I could not say no to Pat, who found places to send me all over the country. When another East Coast engineer needed to take a vacation, Pat asked me to cover for him. The customer was Easthome in Baltimore, Maryland. I flew into BWI and noticed that this airport was super modern, especially compared to San Jose, which consisted mostly of a row of trailers on the tarmac. Perhaps the proximity to Washington, DC had an impact on the amount of money they spent on this airport.

I found Easthome and met the folks there. I didn't have anything specific to do, but I checked out the tester and found that it needed some filters cleaned. Clogged air filters in electronic equipment make the chips run hotter than they should and hot chips fail faster than cool chips. Often, chip manufacturers use a technique called "Burn In" to eliminate early failures by baking the chips at high temperature for several days before retesting them to make sure that all "infant mortality" units are rejected.

I noticed that the Phoenix hard drive desperately needed a filter change. These hard drives take in room air, run it through an "Absolute Filter" which removes virtually every speck of dust so that the drive can be cooled with super clean air. Any speck of dust can cause the heads, flying at microscopic distances over the disks to crash into the disks resulting in a head crash and destruction of all the data.

A few years earlier we suffered a head crash on our system back in San Jose and it was ugly. Shredded aluminum everywhere and all data gone. Luckily we had backed everything up so we could recover. The problem here at Easthome was that they did not have a spare Absolute Filter on site and it was impossible to get one in the time I had remaining on my visit. I warned them that they better get the local engineer to do a filter change soon. I noted this maintenance issue in an email to Tech Support so they knew that it had been observed.

I also asked the Easthome guys if they had backed up their software and they admitted they hadn't. Luckily for them I had been working on a backup utility that copied the entire hard drive onto the Kennedy reel-to reel tape drive. This is the type of tape drive you see in old movies and TV shows that feature computers. The *Time Tunnel* computer room had a whole bank of them.

The backup procedure was very complex so most people just didn't do it. My new tape drive backup utility covered all the bases and made a backup a no-brainer. I installed the program on an 8 inch floppy and showed them how to use it. I also installed another program I wrote called PMMaster which allowed the maintenance people to keep track of filter changes and other preventive maintenance tasks. It was a very clever program that scanned the tester registers so it could create a list of resources that needed to be maintained. Then any time a maintenance person logged into the system it would check the current date and check to see if any maintenance tasks needed to be done. If so, it gave them a list of things to do and when complete, log back in and check off the items done.

Easthome was very happy with my work there and I enjoyed my time off there because of the proximity to Washington, DC. Over the weekend I took a drive to DC and got a look at all the monuments. The next day I went to Baltimore and visited the Inner Harbor which was a very beautiful tourist attraction. However, it became obvious that you didn't want to venture more than a couple of blocks from the harbor because the surrounding "hood" was a very dangerous place to go, based on the nightly news reports I watched on local TV. After that I stayed close to Easthome lest I find myself in a very bad situation.

After two weeks I was allowed to go home and went back to normal life. A couple of weeks later I got a phone call. It was one of the Easthome guys: Their hard drive crashed (told you) and he wanted to know how to use the Restore option of my Tape Backup program that I had given them. I helped him get through the restore process which wasn't that difficult. Then I used email to let the tech support community know that the Easthome disk drive crashed due to the RadChek maintenance guy ignoring my advice to change out the Absolute Filter in the hard drive. That did it! Little did I know that he was (of course) copied on this email and he flew off the handle at my accusation, innocently worded, but still, it glaringly showed that the disk crash was the result of him shirking his duty and ignoring my recommendation. His email response was as spectacular as it was brief. "Fuck Dan Bullard, I quit!"

He did too. For three months he tried to make a go of it as a carpenter but couldn't live on the sparse income compared to what a field service engineer made, so he came crawling back to RadChek who took him back and restored his seniority. I didn't mean to cause him so much grief, but his sloth resulted in the destruction of a $20,000 hard drive and would have resulted in the loss of all the customer's programs and data had I not given them the tape backup program. I was a little more circumspect in my emails after that, but I was not to blame for his mistake, he was and I offered no apologies for what I did.

Once I got a really great opportunity to get a peek at the life of civil servants. Custer Air Force Base in Sacramento, California bought the most expensive RC18 tester ever built at $4.2 million and needed training on it. I didn't have any trouble getting clearance to get into the complex since I previously served in the U.S. Navy with a Secret security clearance. I did have to rent a car to make the drive from San Jose to Sacramento because my normal commute vehicle was my Suzuki 650 Tempter motorcycle. I drove up to Sacramento early Monday morning, taught the class for the first day and realized that I had left something really important back in San Jose. I drove back down to the RadChek office and picked it up, then spent the night at home. However, since I had not checked into my hotel in Sacramento, I lost my reservation and was charged for the one night I didn't stay there. Oh well. Instead I found a hotel with a pool several miles out of Sacramento and invited the wife to bring the kids up and stay with me for the duration of the class. That was great because we weren't that far from home, yet it was like a mini-vacation for all of us.

Custer AFB did not actually make chips, nor did they test them. The point of having the world's most expensive tester in the history of the company was to act as a threat aimed directly at companies like Raygunz who made chips for the U.S. military. The government owned the rights to the chip design (such as they were as I found out later working on Raygunz products) and sometimes the government contractors like Raygunz and others would raise the price of a chip knowing full well that the government had no choice but to pay it. However, Custer AFB would then threaten to take over production and testing using the "bluff hardware" such as a mini-fab and test floor in the Onizuka building, named for NASA mission specialist Ellison Onizuka killed in the Challenger disaster. By a strange coincidence that was the same space shuttle Xiaoling had been able to visit on the launch pad when she worked for NASA. Coincidentally, I had seen the Challenger myself on the Fourth of July landing of the space shuttle Columbia at Edward's Air Force Base near Bishop. Challenger was there on top of a 747 headed for Florida. It's a damn small world.

This "bluff hardware" strategy seemed like a crazy idea because if you don't actually make chips and test them, it would be really hard to pick up the ball and run with it and do it cheaper than people who do it every day. It's hard to pay taxes while watching the government waste your money with this kind of foolishness, and I could now see why Dwight D. Eisenhower made those statements in his farewell address about the Military-Industrial Complex.

The course went well though. I would drive from the hotel to Sacramento every day, teach the civil servants who did nothing more than present a threat to the likes of Raygunz, General Dynamics and others, and then go back to the hotel where the wife and kids spent all day in the pool.

One day I was driving up the freeway in Sacramento to start another day with the class and I noticed smoke ahead. A driver must have tossed a cigarette out his car window and started the dry grass median on fire. No big deal really, except for one small thing. A CalTrans worker was mowing the grass in the median strip and now he's desperately trying to outrun the fire, "on his six" as the Air Force guys might have said. The mower was pretty slow, and the fire was catching up to him fast. He was in a panic because the only escape route for him would be to drive his super slow mower into the freeway traffic that was coming at him at around 60MPH. I felt bad for the guy, but I couldn't figure out a better solution for him. I hope he survived!

After about a week into this two week programming class, some of the students approached me on a break. They told me that I was working them **too hard**. It's true, I was a stickler for classroom participation, for making students do their labs and reading along with me out of the various manuals. They complained that they had never worked so hard in their entire careers, even college was easier than what I was putting them through. I found this last statement extremely hilarious because not long before that, two of my students approached me on a break and told me that my instructional method was better than anything they had ever gotten in college.

I didn't laugh in their faces, but I did chide them a bit. I let them know that in San Jose several customers had sent managers to attend my classes to make sure they weren't a waste of money. After vetting the course (and me) they would often send their best employees to training in my class to give them a bit of a break from the intense working conditions often found in Silicon Valley. Most of my private sector customers considered my training class to be a bit of a vacation. In one case, Rotomolded expected their employees to put in a full day of work after attending a full day of training in my class.

I continued to work them at the normal pace, and, as was my custom, reminded them that they would only get a diploma if they completed the final laboratory exercise. Yes, I guess I was a hard ass, but here I am paying the taxes that pay these guys' salaries for life and they want to breeze through my class without putting in at least as much work as I am in training them? Forget it!

When I made the move from RadChek to Steppenwolf I had to get used to a different crowd of people, but on one trip I had what amounted to a reunion with my old friends at RadChek.

I was in the San Jose airport at 5AM getting set to fly down to San Diego to visit Southern Morse who owned both digital and analog testers made by Steppenwolf. In the gate area I saw my old friend Connie who was a very bright female engineer, but I noticed she was in the bar guzzling a Michelob beer first thing in the morning. This seemed totally out of character, Connie is a great person, a very smart lady and a super fast talker. She didn't strike me as an alcoholic at all. After her second beer I asked why she was drinking beer first thing in the morning. Her reply was that she was scared to death of flying and needed a couple of good jolts to have enough courage to get on the plane. As it turned out we were both flying down to San Diego. RadChek was having a Users Group meeting and so all my old friends would be there. We checked with the gate agent to see if we could be seated together so I could help her with the "ordeal" of takeoff and flight and they were able to comply. Once on the plane Connie asked if she could clutch my arm during takeoff, admitting that she had done this with complete strangers in the past and no one ever refused. OK, I said, better with a friend than with a stranger!

We got lined up on the runway and the pilot spun up the turbines. Boy, did she have a grip! I wondered what the strangers she had flown with thought of this situation! Once in the air she ordered another beer. Wow, I was stunned, I like drinking too, but not first thing in the morning, especially when I have to show up for work at Southern Morse this very morning!

She told me what hotel all the RadChek people would be staying at, so I joined them that evening for dinner. We had a couple of drinks at the hotel before heading off for a place to have dinner, but I forgot that I was not with RadChek anymore and while everyone else's drinks were paid for, I was chased down to pay for my drinks, since RadChek was not going to pay for the drinks of a competitor. "Honest, I'm not trying drink and dash!"

Southern Morse was located on a very beautiful campus in the inland town of Rancho Bernardo, AKA Rancho Relaxo per *The Simpson's* TV show. I was there to teach a two week SOS3000 mixed signal training course to many very skilled mixed signal trained engineers. I previously met a couple of people from here when I was first trained on the system back in San Jose, but now it was me doing the training and I was a bit green. Still, I did a passable job teaching the class and handling other issues as they came up.

Two new testers arrived while I was there and the manager I was reporting to at the time asked if I could install them. Piece of cake I said, I was able to do it over lunch, which really impressed the SM guys. I got through the class with no trouble and found that I really enjoyed the town. The next time SM asked for an onsite class I talked my wife into coming down with me.

We packed the kids into our Chevy Astro and I put my Suzuki 650 Tempter on my trailer and towed it all the way down from San Jose to Rancho Bernardo. Now we had two vehicles; my bike would take me from the hotel to work and my wife and kids would have the Astro to run around the San Diego area. We were both familiar with San Diego since I went to U.S. Navy Boot Camp and BEEp school (Basic Electricity and Electronics) there, and my wife had attended Navy Radioman school there. It was like a vacation for them. It was still work for me, but at least I wasn't down there all alone. The class went well and we all had a great time. At the end of the class I loaded my motorcycle back on the trailer and we drove up to Los Angeles and spent a day at Disneyland before heading back to San Jose. It was brilliant! This was the way to travel!

One way to **not** travel came immediately after my trip to Hong Kong. Just before I headed off to Hong Kong I got a request to give an Operators Training class at Southern Morse. However, I had no idea what that was. I had not been trained on any such class, I didn't even know if such a class existed. I told my boss, Mike Noyce who had brought me over from RadChek that I had no idea what they wanted and that they wanted the class to occur the week after I got back from Hong Kong. I told him that he had better find someone else to do it, perhaps the local Applications Engineer, Sy Johnson. The problem was the Mike was a really crappy manager. He ignored anything I told him, and then he would ignore any memos I sent him. He admitted that when his inbox got too full, he just dumped it all in the trash. If someone really needed something, they would come straight to him and then he might deal with it. Brilliant!

So the Saturday that I returned from two weeks in Hong Kong, I drove to the Steppenwolf office just to check on the status of this trip. I looked in my cubicle and found an airplane ticket to San Diego for the next day, Sunday sitting on my chair. I hadn't been home for an hour yet and I would be getting on another plane the next day to teach a class I had no idea how to teach or even what to use for materials. I was devastated. I missed my family like crazy, but I was just going to be sent straight back out with only one night to wind down from a very eventful trip to Hong Kong. I was not a happy camper.

So after a sleepless night, my wife and kids saw me off at the airport again, but at least it was only a week and in the good old U.S.A.
I tried to figure out what I could teach them. Before I left for Hong Kong I had asked Southern Morse for a copy of their operator procedures and they had complied while I was away. I found their fax sitting in my inbox in the mailroom. I thought maybe I could pull it off, but I was so depressed I drank myself into a stupor that Sunday night missing my family terribly but I pressed on best as I could.

The next day I got to the Southern Morse campus and met with the operations manager, an Indian guy named Mayank Boob (I know, it was hard not to laugh!). When I told him I needed to make transparencies of their operator procedures because that's all the course material I could come up with he flew off the handle. "This is totally unacceptable! We can teach our operators our test procedures! We brought you down here to teach the Steppenwolf Operators Training Course!" I explained that I didn't have anything like that in my possession, which I had tried to tell him on the phone before my Hong Kong trip and didn't know what else to do. I had just gotten back from Hong Kong and was jet-lagged (and hungover, although I left that part out) and was shipped down here without any notice.

Mayank was pissed off. They had scheduled a group of operators to attend my class and now they were here waiting to be trained and I had no materials to train them with. He walked me to the front door and told me he was going to complain loudly to the salesman. After that I didn't know what else to do. I went back to the hotel and tried making some phone calls, but he had beaten me to it and now I was in trouble. It was quite likely I would lose my job. Then I realized that I left my jacket at Southern Morse, so I went back to retrieve it. They let me in and while I couldn't find it (I was so upset and realized later that I hadn't brought one with me) but it turned out that my return was a good thing. Some of the engineers had a technical question on the system so I helped them get the schematics they needed by putting in a desperate phone call to Will Charlatan back in Burlington. So at least I had saved a little face, but I was also told to get my butt back to San Jose for an ass chewing.

I checked out of the hotel and caught a flight back home. I went into the office on Tuesday fully prepared to be fired. I got a good ass chewing all right, and they assigned someone who wasn't my boss to hear my story to help determine my fate. Luckily management agreed that I wasn't entirely to blame, but of course when your boss gets the blame, he's not going to treat you very well after that. I had a rather tempestuous relationship with him after that and eventually, he got laid off and was replaced by a woman.

As an epilogue to this story, many years later I found a manilla folder in the filing cabinet I had inherited from Sally that contained the SOS3000 Operators Course. Oh well, you can't blame me for not knowing the entire contents of a filing cabinet someone left behind after they quit their job.

On another trip down I was going to be taking a class at Southern Morse instead of teaching one. They wanted a class on how to test Telephone Codecs. Codec is short for Coder-Decoder. This is the chip that digitizes and compresses the microphone input on a landline telephone and decompresses and converts the digital signal to analog for the earpiece. I didn't know squat about codecs so Steppenwolf hired a freelance engineer to give the class and I would be sitting in with the SM employees on this one week class.

The instructor taught us all a lot about mixed signal which was still rather new to me. Then he talked about aliasing, which was not really well understood at the time. Every place I had visited I asked nearly every engineer I could find about aliasing but no one I spoke with on the topic could tell me how to calculate where an alias would fall if it showed up. During the lecture the instructor touted some crazy, convoluted method of calculating the frequency of the aliasing frequency, but it just felt cumbersome. Suddenly I had an epiphany and TA-DA! I had the formula! It was simple and brilliant. I named the two statements that solved the alias location Dan's Aliasing Rules and taught it far and wide throughout my whole career. Thanks to a great Steppenwolf software engineer, Abe Beatty my rules were incorporated into the system software so now Dan's Rules run on thousands of testers millions of times a day all over the world.

One day while in San Jose, this time working for Slumburger I ran into my old friend Dick Holmes who had worked as a contractor teaching mixed signal for Steppenwolf and others. Over the years Dick and I developed a friendship and I taught him all I could about mixed signal, including Dan's Rules for solving aliases. I was happy to help him any way I could. After all, if he hadn't been giving training in foreign lands, I would have to!

So now Dick is teaching mixed signal to Slumburger applications engineers and being paid very well for doing it. I stopped by the classroom to see how it was going when I was stunned into disbelief. He was teaching Dan's Rules, but he didn't call them that. He gave me no credit at all for these very valuable aliasing rules that I had come up with on my own. No one in the whole world had ever figured out this formula and here is Dick virtually taking credit for my invention. I was pissed off, but Dick told me he would not give me credit, it was "Public Domain" since I had trained him without a nondisclosure agreement between us. That ended our friendship and I became more motivated to claim credit for my invention. I hate getting ripped off for my brilliant work, especially something that I had taught to Dick with the expectation that he would at least give me credit for. I mean, how hard is it to say, "I know this guy who came up with this really cool way to solve aliasing." It gives the instructor credence by associating with smart people who invent things.

TerRants requested a mixed signal training class at their plant in Albuquerque New Mexico and I was up on deck. We figured out a way to dump the kids with my parents so April could come with me for the duration of this one week class. As we flew into ABQ, looking out the window I saw what looked like a volcano caldera on the ground and noted the location relative to I-40 going west to Phoenix. After checking into our hotel room, we jumped in the car and drove out to the area where I remembered seeing this interesting geological feature. We got out there around dusk and I could not believe my eyes! Smoldering near the caldera was a glob of lava glowing red from the volcanic heat! We got out to get a closer look and realized it was really just the glowing embers of a campfire someone had left burning! However, the caldera is real, it's west of town near Rio Puerco.

Since we arrived on Friday night, we had the whole weekend, which happened to be the weekend of the Balloon Fiesta, to run around and explore the area. We drove up to Santa Fe and went to quite a few museums. Then we drove out to Los Alamos where the Manhattan Project was based. The lab is still there, many no-trespassing signs and locked gates. We came across a huge herd of Elk blocking the road in the mountains of the Valles Caldera National Reserve.

On Sunday we drove up the back side of Sandia Peak, which towers over the city of Albuquerque from a height of 10,378 feet. As we drove the rental car up the road to the peak, we noticed the altitude markers go up and up and up. At the summit we got out of the car feeling great, thinking, hey, 10,000 feet? No problem! There were some stairs leading to a vista point on the peak, and every 10 steps was a concrete bench. "Oh yeah, for the wussies" we thought. A few steps up the stairway and we nearly passed out! The air was very thin, and while sitting in the car presented no challenge at this altitude, climbing stairs or walking any distance certainly did! We enjoyed the fabulous view of the city 5,000 feet below and then went back down to catch our breath and get ready for the upcoming work week.

The class was super smooth. The students were knowledgeable, friendly and helpful in the classroom and the lab. Later I got word that they were quite pleased with the training. I just wish I had realized that the city itself was at 5,000 feet elevation. It took me days to figure out why I was so winded carrying my document case, admittedly a heavy load stuffed with books through the parking lot up to the TerRants building.

New destinations was one thing, but traveling to San Jose was not a treat for me. I was not fond of traveling there alone after I moved my family to Oregon. Our move came about because of travel. Steppenwolf was still on the acquisition kick, picking up companies left and right. Eventually they made an offer on the test division of TerroDacNix which had better things to do than make testers. I was asked to go to Beaverton, Oregon to learn their digital tester, the LT1000 (LT for Logic Tester) and see what was going on with a new mixed signal variant, the MT1000 (MT for Mixed-signal Tester). I was to be up there for four weeks, a long haul for me, and no intervening weekend home. I spent the first two weeks in the programming class as a student, and the last two weeks as a co-instructor, teaching only the parts of the course I was comfortable with.

The good news was that a whole bunch of us Steppenwolf guys were to be trained together, so I had a gaggle of friends with me. Buck Fry was there, along with his secret stash of pot he smuggled on the plane from Austin. Also there was Vince Franklin, with whom I had worked at RadChek, and several other guys I really enjoyed working with.

We all stayed in an Embassy Suites in Beaverton, so every night after class we would meet in the lobby for three hours of free beer with chips and salsa, which I swear they must have bought by the 55 gallon drum. Since all the TerroDacNix guys knew we were staying there, they would accompany us to the hotel and partake in the free happy hour beer bash. The hotel didn't make you show your room key, it seemed that anyone who walked in the front door could partake in the free beer and wine.

I met more TerroDacNix folks and finally met the guy who was the "father" of the new mixed signal tester, Ford Stob. Ford and I had a pleasant chat and I picked up on this new machine very quickly. However, it was apparent that the other folks there were very intimidated by Ford. He was very smart and rather short with people who couldn't keep up. He had a handshake like a pair of Vise-Grip pliers. Years later at a Christmas party, I introduced April to Ford. I warned her that he had a viselike handshake, so during her handshake with him she initiated a blood stanching grip in advance and really impressed him.

My Steppenwolf friends and I had fun on the weekend and after work. I came to really love Beaverton, or Beavertron they call it for all the electronics companies that sprang up around TerroDacNix. I started my third week there alone, my friends had all been trained and went back home, while I had to stay and co-teach the course I just went through. We had a classroom full of new students, and one of them was a former U.S. Navy Chief from RotoMolded named Mike. We got to be good friends, especially because the instructor of the training class, Jim Jones spoke a really crazy version of *tester talk*. For example, he would say **reed** instead of relay, or **single** instead of signal. It was a very strange speech impediment that made it hard for people who already had a background in testers to understand what he was talking about.

So during the class, I would sit behind Mike and translate for him. When Jim would say, "reed" I would say, "relay" and when Jim would say, "FICM" I would translate, "Local Memory." It worked out well.

One day the instructor, Jim started teaching us how to use the tester software libraries and Mike flew off the handle! He had seen many problems at RotoMolded because of people using software libraries that stood alone without much documentation about how they worked. He was upset at Jim's response to his objection, so I promised to talk with someone who would listen to his concerns. You don't just shrug off the concerns of a major customer like RotoMolded. They were a major player and could make or break your company.

The class went by, day by day, but the problem was I was getting lonely and now the wife and I were fighting over the phone about some stupid thing and it was just too much hassle. After three and a half weeks I said goodbye to Mike, checked out of the hotel and caught a flight home. I didn't get in trouble for leaving early, which was a relief, and the wife and I were able to patch things up quickly. However, I was quite fascinated with Oregon and thought it might be a good place to live someday.

Then we got our chance: Steppenwolf was looking for ways to save money, and one way would be for us to combine our training centers in San Jose and Beaverton into one facility. Where should it be? The guys in Oregon threatened to quit if we asked them to move to California, but my fellow trainer in San Jose, Tom Gregory had lived and worked in Beaverton for a few years when he was assigned to support HiQ. He raved about how great Oregon was. The housing was much cheaper, the schools were better, the climate was wet but that made it greener than dry, dusty old California which seemed to be in a constant state of drought.

We worked on a presentation, our boss gave it to the board, and it worked! We were transplanted to Oregon. The company flew my wife and I up to Portland on a house hunting trip and we found a place we really liked for one-third less than our San Jose house would bring, and it was almost twice the size to boot! We got the paperwork going, but the problem was, I was still traveling like a mad man.

I got power-of-attorney for my wife, and my wife got power-of-attorney for me, so we could sign for each other. I was teaching a class in Beaverton at the time the home purchase in Oregon was going forward, so I dealt with the paperwork there, while my wife took care of selling our home in San Jose. This was really tricky because we scheduled our move date for the day I got back from Oregon from yet another training course up there. I flew back to San Jose to an empty house and all five of us slept in sleeping bags on air mattresses for our last night on Rhapsody Way. The next day we loaded up the Astro van and drove it with our sailboat trailing behind us to Beaverton.

We stayed in the same old Embassy Suites for two nights, then just two days before Christmas moved into our new house in Aloha just outside of Beaverton. We enjoyed a quiet Christmas, complete with a little snow and then, I was back on the road again, this time to... San Jose! I had two, two week training courses scheduled in San Jose with a one week break between the two. My manager was somewhat sympathetic so she let me take that intervening week off so I could finish moving us into the new house. However, it seemed to me like moving to Oregon was not going to reduce my travel, it was just going to reverse the direction and make me a visitor in my old hometown.

From then on, every time I had to go to San Jose I would fall into a deep melancholy as I drove down roads that reminded me of my family. I tried to confront the problem head on by going to Orchard Supply Hardware where I had spent many happy hours with my son browsing the aisles for hardware to build go-karts or teeter-totters or other things that we had fun constructing together. It just made me sadder. I would drive past places I had taken the kids bike riding or parks we had visited while we lived there. It was just way too much for me to handle without my family and it just made me miss them even more. I was not made for bachelor life, at least since I had a family.

Still, San Jose is where Silicon Valley is, and I had to make many, many trips down there. I gave a training class in San Jose at a company named TTH, which was short for The Test House where I met a guy named Mark Mertens. Mark had worked for TerroDacNix in Oregon years ago, but got laid off and had to move to San Jose and take a job with TTH. The poor guy had to sign a virtual indentured servitude contract with the owner of the business, an Arab immigrant. More grating was the fact that Mark was a U.S. veteran, which meant he had served America, yet he was enslaved in his own country by an immigrant who saw nothing wrong with mistreating a natural born U.S. military veteran. Absolutely horrific.

When I finally had my fill of travel at Steppenwolf I applied for and got a job at Slumburger who wanted me to be the local applications engineer at HiQ in Hillsboro, Oregon, just down the road from my home in Aloha. However, to get up to speed on their tester, the S9000 series, I had to go to San Jose for five weeks of training. All my friends (so called) at Steppenwolf thought it was pretty funny that immediately after quitting my job at Steppenwolf because of travel, I had to travel for five whole weeks, when Steppenwolf had promised to knock off the travel just to keep me.

Nevertheless I found it was a good move, despite all that time away from home. I was able to work on testers at one of the best semiconductor facilities in the U.S., probably the best in the world and certainly the most recognizable to the general population. Everyone knows who HiQ is, they are pretty much the only semiconductor company that runs ads on TV.

After working at HiQ for a few months my boss sent me down to San Jose for a one week training class on the EXA tester, a mixed signal tester in the Slumburger S9000 line. A really great thing about this trip was that this time I was able to bring my wife and kids. Since this was after we moved to Oregon, we drove down to California and dropped the kids off at my folks' place in West Point. April and I then drove the rest of the way down to San Jose and had a bit of a getaway together in our old hometown.

At this point I was an expert at mixed signal, but apparently the instructor of this class was not. Poor guy, I felt really bad for him stumbling through the material (been there, done that). I kept interjecting helpful points along the way in the class but instead of helping him, it just made him more self conscious. Interestingly there was a guy in the class who I previously had a run-in with many years earlier. Leroy had given me grief the first time we met because I was trying to teach the SOS6000 class for the first time and I was a little wobbly on the tester. However, now I was an expert at mixed signal and Leroy was new to it, so our roles were reversed and he was sucking up to me a bit. It was quite embarrassing!

So as this poor Slumburger instructor stumbled and stammered through the material, I came up with a plan. I told him I would leave the class on Thursday, a full day early if he let me give a lecture that showed the utility of DSP, the stuff he was teaching the class about. After my lecture he could give me my diploma and I would get out of his hair. He agreed. I gave a two hour lecture on a technique I used recently for another customer, got my diploma and April and I took off for West Point a full day early, avoiding the Friday rush to get out of the Bay Area.

One of my most successful trips to San Jose started in a hotel in Taiwan. While sitting in my hotel room after meeting with a customer I began to work out a way to use our cheap little tester to measure very high frequencies. Usually, measuring high frequencies means buying an external instrument from a third party vendor and then hooking it into the system, a messy, expensive and error prone way to do things. Invariably the third party vendor will change the model shortly after you get everything working, only to make your new solution obsolete and unsupportable, requiring more work to integrate the new model of their, now more expensive unit into the test solution. Instead I formulated a clever way to measure frequency using only what we had in our tester. It was based purely on mathematics and was quite clever. When I got back home I coded it and sure enough, it worked! I beat my new algorithm (geek speak for solution) to death to make sure it was robust, filled all the holes I came across with even more brilliant solutions and wrote it up as an applications note that would be disseminated to our customer base and potential customers to show that we can come up with brilliant solutions to their test problems. That's how you win customers in the test biz.Well, that and taking them to strip clubs.

I sent the applications note to my old buddy Malcolm Reynolds who had since relocated to New Hampshire, to see what he thought, since he was far smarter than I on all things mathematical. A few days later I got a call from him. "You stole my idea!" he claimed. It turns out, he had been struggling with a similar problem and came up with the same solution. He had emailed it to me weeks earlier, but it looked like unintelligible drivel to me at the time, so I just ignored it. However, because we talked about stuff like this often and faced the same problems using the same methods, we had accidentally co-invented a new technique for measuring frequency. Mine was more robust because I had implemented it whereas his paper explored the theoretical side of the problem.

We decided to name it the Bullard-Reynolds Frequency Measure Technique and I made him a coauthor of the applications note. After all, he was the co-inventor. I passed the applications note on to Contessa Beatle, our corporate communications lady, who had already gotten me published in the magazine Evaluation Engineering with my article on testing filters using Periodic White Noise (also co-authored by Malcolm). Contessa found a way to get it into the magazine Test and Measurement World, so now Malcolm and I were published again.

I was able to visit Malcolm and his colleague Jean St. James in Meredith, New Hampshire on Lake Winnipesaukee, the subject of the film *On Golden Pond* with Henry Fonda and Katherine Hepburn. I combined it with a visit to Farewell-Honeychild, a merger between those two world famous companies that had a facility in Portland, Maine, the namesake of Portland, Oregon. Jean had a huge home on the shoreline of a neighboring lake, Lake Waukewan, with his own private boat dock. We were able to discuss a number of issues including our cool new frequency measurement technique. Afterwards I drove across New Hampshire and Maine directly to Portland and had a meeting with Farewell-Honeychild to discuss our attempts to woo them into our customer base. Unfortunately, even though we put a lot of effort into that sale, it never materialized, mostly because I was busy with Traxite in San Jose and Red Stevens apparently didn't take them to enough strip clubs.

One day I received a call from my old buddy Helmut Gibson, an older sales guy with whom I really enjoyed working. Helmut was courting a potential customer, Wacon in San Jose that needed to measure very high frequencies. Except for that one issue, the TestEz machine was perfectly suited to everything they needed it for. He had already given them some reprints of my article that Contessa had gotten from T&M World. They found it intriguing, but they really didn't believe it, since none of them had ever heard of this technique before. Well, **duh**, it's brand new people!

I asked Helmut if it would help us get our tester in the door if I developed a one day seminar on the technique, complete with a lab exercise so they could see it work for themselves. He thought that was a great idea. I spent a week developing the course, we scheduled it and I flew down to San Jose to give a one day class. I won't need to tell you how it went after I tell you that the next day Wacon signed a purchase order for 10 systems at $400,000 each.

I was on fire at TestEz, I kept doing better and better work. I was especially good at developing trade show demos. A nifty demo I did for the

International Test Conference (ITC) in Charlotte, North Carolina was based on an idea my boss, Mick Archangel came up with. He wanted me to build a demo that would measure the speed of some object by its Doppler Shift using the tester. I figured out how to use the built-in instruments to measure the Doppler Shift using a Fast Fourier Transform (FFT). Then I built many different versions, including a football, a baseball, a remote control car, but we eventually decided to use a train for the demo based on Mick's theme of "TestEz, your Light at the End of the Tunnel." The tunnel was the very dark times after the 2001 terrorist attacks and the resulting economic recession. Companies were going belly up left and right, people were losing their jobs, going bankrupt, etcetera. It was really scary and it lasted for about 2 years.

The idea behind his theme was that you hoped the light at the end of the tunnel was not an oncoming train. He contracted a trade show booth maker to build a giant replica of a tunnel and I played the part of the "Light" in a white tuxedo, including white shoes. It was fantastic! The demo worked like a charm and one guy came up to me during the show to tell me it was the best demo he had ever seen in his twenty plus years of attending ITC.

That was consolation for spending a week in Charlotte wearing a rented white tuxedo to the show every day. However, I must say, I was never treated better, by coworkers or just random strangers. People would open doors for me, move aside politely to let me pass in crowded areas or just stop talking and show deference as I passed. Even the CEO, Bob Hood was being super gracious. At the end of one day I picked up my laptop bag to sling it over my shoulder and Bob yanked it out of my hands and carried it for me, even though he was also carrying his own bag. I told him I could carry it, but he retorted, "Dan, you've put in a long day, you deserve a break." That was so awesome! I had become the symbol of TestEz at the show (since I stood out like a sore thumb in my glaringly white tux), and Bob, being the CEO realized that how they treated me in public would tell the attendees how they treated "the talent." It wouldn't do for the attendees or the competitors to see **the guy in the white tux** carrying his own **black** laptop bag. I wasn't a bellboy, I was Mr. TestEz and I deserved respect from even the CEO of the company. Lesson learned: You want to be treated well? Dress well. Even complete strangers will open doors for you.

It even got me out of a rather humiliating job, sign holder at ITC. Mick, who always had great ideas for trade shows arranged to have show attendees bussed over to an indoor race track for an evening of go-cart racing. Since this was NASCAR country it was sure to be a hit. Someone gave me a big sign pointing the way to the bus so the customers could find their way and asked me to direct customers to the bus. I looked ridiculous standing there in a white tux holding a sign, but it was a good idea, because I was the talk of the show, everyone knew I was the TestEz guy. Thankfully the Asian salesman, Lam Thong came along and said, "Dan, you look like Colonel Sanders, put that sign down and go change clothes for the race event." Thank you Lam! Only an Asian would understand, since the only guy they have ever seen in a white tux stands outside Kentucky Fried Chicken restaurants all over Asia holding a sign inducing people to come in and eat Finger Lickin' Good™ chicken.

For some reason, TestEz kept trying to get me to down to San Jose and spend weeks away from home, but without any real project in mind. The sales guy that had taken me to LogAnaChip in Boston, George McFly asked me to come down to spend some time in San Jose, presumably so that the aura of my intelligence would raise the overall IQ of the facility. I came up with a compromise and told him I would be happy to drive down in a rental car if I could swing by my parent's ranch in West Point, then drive down to San Jose to do his bidding. He agreed and so I rented a car, drove down and eventually showed up in San Jose.

I really didn't have anything to do, but I chatted with some of the applications engineers, gave some informal training classes and looked at some issues George thought I should work on. I confronted George about making me stay in San Jose for no good reason, but he reminded me I was only a couple of hours from home in Portland. Sure, a couple of hours, but are you going to let me fly home tonight, then fly back tomorrow, then fly home again tomorrow night? No? Well then stop making it sound like I can go home any time I want!

George had to fly somewhere else, but told me he would check in occasionally to make sure it was going well. After a few days I realized this was all a big waste of time. These guys were not going to absorb mixed signal testing by osmosis, no matter how long I stayed there. Realizing that even though George was acting like my boss, in fact my real boss, Mick would sign my expense report pretty much no matter what I did. I decided it was time to go home without George's permission. I slipped out with little fanfare, jumped in the rental car and started driving back to Portland, Oregon, a twelve hour drive.

I got as far as Davis, near Sacramento when my phone rang. It was George checking up on me. Oh, crap! Had someone told him I left? He asked how it was going. I told him, "I'm making really good progress, really moving along." Of course I was referring to my progress on my drive, but I waited to hear if he had deduced that I was no longer in San Jose. After a few seconds it became clear he thought I was still in San Jose and was working on some project or another. We exchanged goodbyes and I sighed with relief. He was none the wiser, and by the time he figured out what I had done I would be so far away from San Jose that he couldn't ask me to come back. Ten hours later I got home, and the next day he called and asked again, how's it going? "Great!" I replied, "I'm back home and really enjoying myself up here in Portland."

George backed off a bit, but he eventually found a way to keep me in San Jose. He asked me to fly down and attend a meeting with Rod Reardon, the director of test at Traxite in San Jose. They were making and testing chips that go into TV sets and cable/satTV set-top boxes. Rod gave us a chip that we could try to test. It required *laser trim* which was new to me and everyone at TestEz. I had to get up to speed on the laser trimmer, which is fairly simple to understand. The idea is that we would test something on the chip, the measurement would tell us which component on the chip to burn with the laser. Then we'd zap it with the laser, test it again to make sure the laser had done its job, and then move on to the next test. However, it would require me to be in San Jose for months at a time because they weren't going to lend me a laser trimmer of my own in Portland. I agreed that I would fly down on Monday and fly home on Thursday every week until the project was done. It took months, but I got it to work to Traxite's satisfaction and really impressed Rod with my work ethic and technical savvy. During a meeting I mentioned that I was wasting a lot of time sitting in my rental car in the parking lot listening to Rush Limbaugh on the car radio while waiting for the laser trimmer to finish running other products. Rod quickly found me an office to use in the building to make me more available to the other Traxite folks who might have questions about the TestEz tester. *God forbid Dan become a frothy mouthed right winger right here in our parking lot!*

The thing that sort of bothered me about all this travel is that TestEz employed a whole building full of applications engineers, with degrees no less, sitting around in San Jose doing...what? Why couldn't they assign one of those guys to work at Traxite? At least assign someone to be my understudy to help me get Traxite up to speed on our system. After all, I had been hired as the Marketing guy! Apparently all these TestEz folks were scared to death of mixed signal. I remember giving a lecture at a sales meeting and having to explain histograms. Anyone who has an engineering degree should know what a histogram is! Ever seen a Bell Curve? That's a histogram. Although I didn't have a degree, I had invented a histogram for testing my random number generator to make sure my slot machine game was truly random! Perhaps instead of getting degrees, these guys should have screwed off writing game programs on company time. They might have learned something about computer science, math and number theory.

It didn't work out that way. I got Traxite up to speed all by myself and they handed us a big order based purely on my work. I would have been happy to share the credit, but no one stepped up to help, so I took all the credit for myself! I was rewarded at the annual sales meeting with a bottle of wine. I thought everyone knew I had since given up drinking. Oh well.

Once I won the order at Traxite I was allowed to stop the weekly shuttle to San Jose, except for the occasional training class to get all the Traxite guys up to speed on this new tester. One class had to be given in a hotel in San Jose, as the classroom at TestEz was being used for a digital class. George helped me out by dropping off the tester and ten computer workstations in the hotel lobby and then driving away in the predawn light. I got to install all the computers and the tester and assemble the manuals in the hotel conference room before the students showed up. I kind of felt like George ditched me to make my life even more miserable, but at least having the class in the hotel gave it a more elegant air, and meant I had no commute! I could even retire to my hotel room on a break if I felt like it.

To sweeten the success of this new order, the Traxite guys were really enjoying my training and reported back to their bosses what a great trainer I was. This was a huge boon for my status in TestEz and Traxite alike.

Because I was getting orders and blowing away customers left and right, I now had enough clout that I could book my own travel and choose my own hotels and rental car company. After all the other rental car places had screwed me, Avis was the only rental car company I would use. While I was winning the business at Traxite, the Pakistani guy at the Avis lot knew me so well he would greet me the same way every Monday morning. "Hello Mr. Dan, how are you today? Thank you, see you next Monday!" Oh my God, my life had become so predictably boring even a Pakistani stranger knew when and where I would be every Monday morning. It was disgusting, but there was no way out. I had kids in college, two mortgages on the house in Oregon, *livin' on money that I ain't made yet*[1] and I was not going to be able to escape. Would I ever be able to *slow down and live my life full measure?* Not yet, but someday. Someday.

---

[1] From the song Five O'clock World by The Vogues

Up every mornin' just to keep a job
I gotta fight my way through the hustlin' mob
Sounds of the city poundin' in my brain
While another day goes down the drain

But it's a five O'clock world when the whistle blows
No one owns a piece of my time
And there's a five O'clock me inside my clothes
Thinkin' that the world looks fine, yeah

Tradin' my time for the pay I get
Livin' on money that I ain't made yet
Gotta keep goin', gotta make my way
While I live for the end of the day

Cuz it's a five O'clock world when the whistle blows
No one owns a piece of my time
And there's a long-haired girl who waits, I know
To ease my troubled mind, yeah

In the shelter of her arms everything's OK
She talks and the world goes slippin' away
And I know the reason I can still go on
When every other reason is gone,

In my five O'clock world she waits for me
Nothing else matters at all
Cuz every time my baby smiles at me
I know that it's all worthwhile, yeah
Five O'clock World by The Vogues

Taiwan

"And now for our missile report,... I mean traffic report"
ICRT radio announcer during the 1995 Chinese missile launches over Taiwan

I have been to Taiwan almost twenty times, as counted by the stamps in my passport. Look at the cover, right now, you'll find a few. So many memories, and so many interesting stories, where to begin?

I had been to Hong Kong before and assumed that Taiwan wouldn't be that much different, both places are populated mostly with Han Chinese people. There were also indigenous people on the island of Formosa which is Portuguese for "beautiful island." It is very lovely in some ways. Plants grow like crazy there, so it looks like a garden. Thank God, too! The plants hide all the garbage laying about. Don't cut the grass, you never know what is hiding down there!

Taiwan became home to many Chinese after Chiang Kai-shek lost the war with Mao and his communist buddies for control of Mainland China. CKS took all the gold, money, warships and other important possessions of his government to Taiwan to reestablish the Chinese government in exile. For the longest time the U.S. only recognized the government in Taiwan as the legitimate government of China. Richard Nixon normalized relations in 1972 and was the first U.S. President to visit Mainland China.

Still, Taiwan remains a good friend of the U.S., and surprisingly Japan. While the Japanese held Korea, China and Taiwan during World War II, the Taiwanese got over it, the Chinese and Koreans never did. The Taiwanese put their feelings about the Japanese occupation aside to make money from them. I found almost no resentment of Japan when in Taiwan, not so in Korea or China. In Taiwan making money was paramount and the latest incarnation of money making enterprises was chip testing, my specialty.

My first trip to Taiwan was to help my old buddy, So Ree Jack teach a class on mixed signal testing and visit a few customers who bought our equipment in the Free Trade Zone in the city of Kaohsiung, (pronounced cow-shung, or mockingly called cow-dung) in the south of Taiwan.

To get to Kaohsiung you have to fly into Taipei's Chiang Kai-shek international airport and then catch a transfer flight to Kaohsiung airport, which later became an international airport in its own right.

Arriving in Kaohsiung I caught a cab to my hotel, The Grand Palm, a smallish place with a wide open lobby, no doors, just walk in. I thought, gee, must be warm here all the time, kind of like Hawaii where many of the public buildings also have no doors. I was wrong, but not about the weather. I was wrong about the doors.

The staff were very cordial, I rode the elevator to my room, and was instructed how the room lights worked. In most of Asia the hotels have a "fob" on the room key that you place into a niche near the door that turns on all the power in the room. Take the keys out, and all power in the room goes off. It helped save on power for the hotel. Good idea, I thought.

I noticed this strange smell, I couldn't quite place it. It sort smelled like the aftermath of my high school days when I would drink too much homemade wine. That was it, it smelled like bile, that nasty smell you get when you have been throwing up all night. I was hoping it would go away. It didn't. It seems that most Asian hotel designers don't include P-traps in the sewage fixtures. So all the sewer gas that accumulates just rises through the fixtures, the sink, the floor drain, whatever.

However, the place had a bed, and a roof, and a window. Near the window was this odd looking rope ladder. I read the instructions. It seemed that in case of a fire, you should open the window, toss the ladder out the window and climb down to the ground. I looked out the window, there were power lines going by, supplying power to all the business on this street. Oh, but they had thought of that, they placed plastic sleeves over the wires so you wouldn't get electrocuted when you climbed down. Good idea, I sure hope it can hold back the 8,000 volts coursing through those wires. I wasn't interested in testing that theory, so I hoped there would be no fires.

At breakfast the next morning I tried the buffet, cold scrambled eggs, hmmm. I found out several days later that they were supposed to be hot, but the warmer for the scrambled egg bin had crapped out. No one noticed for, how long? No idea, but they eventually got it fixed. At least they had bacon, and a very strange bread for toast. They weren't very good at making bread, not really a Chinese thing anyway.

I was picked up by one of the Proxsi guys. Proxsi was our rep in Taiwan and they did a hell of a good job selling our testers. It was my job to support them until the Proxsi guys could get up to speed. Right now the only thing they could do was service the systems, they had no programmers, but that would change over time. They were all very friendly guys, much nicer than the Koreans (as you'll see later), with every intent of being helpful and friendly. I could stand this. I always rode to and from work with a Proxsi guy, that was part of their job and they were given car allowances to offset the costs.

Good thing too because driving in Taiwan was very, how can I put this? Chaotic. No one obeyed the rules. People would pull up to a red traffic light, slow down, perhaps even stop! Then again, perhaps not. If they did stop they would soon be swarmed by hundreds of scooters, pulling in front of and alongside the poor car driver. When the light turned green the scooters would roar away belching a cloud of blue two-stroke smoke and the cars would eventually be able to go. All the drivers seemed very skilled at just *barely* clearing each other's vehicles. Cars and scooters gave each other just inches, yet I never saw an accident. People were just plain *rude* but everyone ignored the insults, it was just part of getting around. My favorite Proxiite, Won Hung used to get annoyed sometimes. Nearly everything out of his mouth cracked me up. One time a truck blew through a red light and came right at us, Won slammed on the brakes to let him go past and he exclaimed in the funniest accent "He tried to kill me! Why he want to kill me?" Ask anyone who knows Won, he's a really hilarious guy.

Virtually every customer I visited expected me to change shoes and wear sandals in the building to reduce dirt dragged in from the outside which was filthy, so I understood why. The problem is that Asian feet are much smaller than mine and I could never find sandals that were big enough for my size 11 feet. Wearing these sandals made walking and working very difficult. In some cases we would be pushing very large machines around on raised computer floors of questionable strength. I could see one of these machines run over my toes or the floor collapsing under me. In the U.S. you would be expected to wear steel toed boots to do this kind of work. Doing it with undersized sandals that have been worn by who knows how many people before me just freaked me out.

After a week of teaching, visiting and helping, So Ree suggested I come back with him to Hong Kong for the weekend, it was a better place to stay than Kaohsiung. Fine, that was OK with me, I liked Hong Kong. Not nearly as dirty as Taiwan. I checked out of the hotel, but told them I would be back on Tuesday and flew to Hong Kong with So Ree.

Despite being the weekend, we visited a customer in Hong Kong on Saturday. The customer, a white guy from the States chatted with me about living in Hong Kong with his American wife. He admitted that his wife hated the place. Almost every day he would come home and find his wife crying about some insult from some Chinese person. It could be worse lady, you could be living in Korea! There husbands are allowed to beat their wives, and worse.

When I got back to my hotel in Kaohsiung on Tuesday I noticed something different. The hotel now had doors, big sliding glass doors. As I came into the lobby the clerk remembered me and handed me my room key, I didn't even have to sign in! What service! I asked about the doors, he told me they were new, to replace the old ones that had been "*broking*" by a car smashing through them. Well, that explains everything. I guess I had better watch my step around here.

That is certainly true in Taiwan. Every square inch of sidewalk is taken up with parked scooters. Not only that, the government doesn't build or maintain the sidewalks, each business builds and maintains their own section of sidewalk and the styles, materials and heights vary from storefront to storefront. The junctions between sections of sidewalk can be treacherous, assuming there is enough room among the scooters to walk on the sidewalk. The worst fate anyone could have would to be a blind person trying to walk to the market in Taiwan. You would be dead in a matter of days, either from tripping over a sidewalk junction or getting run over by a car as you tried to get around all the scooters on the sidewalk.

There were open areas, I wouldn't call them parks though. In some places there were empty lots where a building had been torn down or not yet built up. It was either full of dead scooters (scooter heaven I guess) or heaps of trash bags full of trash. After a trip to China I noticed the difference between China and Taiwan. In Taiwan there were empty lots heaped with garbage in black plastic garbage bags. In China, they didn't use bags.

Taiwan was awash in ugly, mutt dogs on the street, trying to make a living. Occasionally you would come across one that had been run over. It wouldn't be there the next day, and although I am not certain where they went I have a theory.

One evening when Won and I had been working all day, well, I worked and Won watched, but anyway... We got out of the customer site after 9PM. It was customary for Won to take me to get something eat and he loved this part of his job. All Taiwanese, and Chinese too, relish eating. I guess it comes from eons of not eating. A common greeting in Chinese countries is "chī fàn le ma?" (吃饭了吗？) which means "Have you eaten?" It's not really an invitation to dinner or anything, it's more like, "How are you doing?" but of course if you haven't eaten in a couple of days, as might have been true in the not too distant past, the answer is likely to be, "not so good!"

Anyway, at 9PM everything is closed, so the only place we can go to get a bite to eat is at a sidewalk vendor. This is a guy who has cleared out enough scooters to make room for his grill, and this one had an extra feature:

He had a dining room in the building behind the grill! So Won ordered me something to eat and a Taiwan Beer. When in a third world country, never drink water and never drink anything with ice. You'll regret it!

The dining room was ankle deep in garbage from other people eating all day, perhaps days. Two feral dogs rooted through the trash to pick out scraps the diners left behind. It was *disgusting.* I just couldn't eat here! Perhaps the food was OK, but the surroundings were so unappetizing, and there was *that smell* again. I grabbed a piece of meat with my chopsticks and waved it toward one of the dogs. He skittishly moved towards me and took the meat from my chopsticks. I fed him and his buddy all my food, except for the hot peppers (that would be a cruel trick). The other "diners" were aghast as they watched me. What the hell was this *Bai Yuan Gong* (white ape man) doing feeding these dogs? I could get by on beer. I think partly because of this, Won didn't allow the customer to keep me beyond 8PM anymore, so we could always go someplace clean, like Crabs House. Not Crab House mind you, Crabs House. Good place, good crab. Don't miss the crab roe, the female crab eggs that stick to the inside of the carapace. Yummy!

The other town I frequented was Hsinchu (Sin Chew). At first Kaohsiung was dirtier than Hsinchu, but over time Kaohsiung got cleaner and even got a few 4 or 5 star hotels. Hsinchu got better over time, but not as fast as Kaohsiung. Hsinchu has a "Science Based Industrial Park" a ways out of town where all the electronics companies were located. To get to Hsinchu you flew into Chiang Kai-shek airport and caught a special cab that would drive you the two hours or so to Hsinchu. Usually these special cabs were hired by Proxsi to meet me at the airport and drive me to the hotel, and when it was time to go they would pick me up wherever I was and take me to CKS. However, since these guys worked for Proxsi and not me, I made it a point to get some business cards from other cabbies who do the long drive to CKS *just in case*. You never know when you are going to need a driver who is loyal to **me**, not Proxsi. It turns out that was a good idea.

While in the States I started getting emails from customer in Kaohsiung that was having an issue. We couldn't seem to figure it out corresponding by email so it was time to go there and look at the problem close up. I setup a two week trip with the boss's OK and flew out the next day. This time I got a great room a the Grand Hai Lai hotel in Kaohsiung, it was fantastic. All pink marble, forty five floors with seven floors below ground that was all shopping, even a supermarket! If I hadn't had to go to work I would never have to leave the hotel! It was so fancy it even had a color TV with remote control in the bathroom! The restaurants were great, the service was great, the price was high, but I wasn't paying and the company allowed me to stay there. How could I pass it up? The Grand Hai Lai was still in Taiwan, and that meant it wasn't perfect but it beat the crap out of the Grand Palm.

One time I was there drinking with a coworker from Oregon, Theo Cleaver in the lobby bar. Theo went to the bathroom, then came back and I said, "OK, my turn." He said, "Be careful!" I wasn't sure what he meant by that but when I got there I found out why I should be careful. Someone had thrown up on the bathroom floor and now that polished pink marble was slicker than snot. I slipped and fell on my back, right into the puke. I was able to get up and do my business, then tried to inform the people at the reception desk about my mishap. They sure were thick, but eventually they got my drift. I rejoined Theo and continued drinking, I could change clothes later and I needed an attitude adjustment after that. Still, the Grand Hai Lai was quite grand, overall.

Won picked me up the next day and took me to the customer site. Almost immediately I figured out what the problem was. I should have figured it out from Portland, but it was just one of those things you had to see, no description in *broking engrish* was going to lead you to the solution. The customer was ecstatic, he was able to make production quota, and I had nothing to do for two weeks! The customer mentioned that the company was throwing a party at the National University of Kaohsiung campus and I was invited, sort of a way to thank me for solving the problem. Wonderful! Free food, free beer, music, sounded like fun, and it was! They had good things to eat like Thai style Chicken Satay, all the Taiwan Beer I could drink and a very interesting venue. There was even an exhibit of Chiang Kai-shek's limousine, his personal car! Now if only every customer could treat me like this!

While I was there, Proxsi decided I should bee-bop around and visit a few customers. I visited one customer after another, gave little seminars, attended meetings, had lunches and so on. One day I was out visiting a customer with a new Proxsi engineer and when lunchtime came he suggested that we go to TerRants, a large semiconductor manufacturer which had a big cafeteria that was free to anyone with an employee or contractor badge. A couple of years earlier I taught a two week class in TerRants and I had eaten in that cafeteria. You stand in line going past a huge pot of rice with a couple of paddles in it. Everyone in line would reach into the pot and scoop out a portion of rice onto their trays. Yuck! How many people had stuck their arm into this pot? Half of these zit faced Asian kids were picking their noses or popping their zits while in line to get some chow. YUCK! When I got to the area where they dished out the main course I was certain to get the most disgusting part of whatever they were serving. If the main course was fish, I would get the head. No use in trying to talk to the servers, they thought that was the best part! I noted that the European manager brought his own lunch to work. Now this young engineer wanted to take me back to TerRants just to get a free lunch! I begged him to take me to a McDonald's, my treat!

After I ran out of things to do in Kaohsiung, Won was told to drive me up to Hsinchu by way of the main North-South highway. This was a riot! First we had to wait for Won's car to get freed up from the parking area. In Taiwan it was common to park your car, bumper-to-bumper blocking in whomever parked their car first. Most drivers would leave the transmission in neutral so that if someone needed to move your car because they blocked you in, you could just shove it around and hopefully not damage it too much. However, the guy that blocked Won's car in had put it in Park. We were stuck. Three hours later, Won's car was unblocked, time to get on the freeway. Four hours of Won driving, I was in stitches! "Why he want to kill me? Why he want to kill me?" The Taiwanese ignored all the laws even on the "freeway." There was no breakdown lane, well, there was but you couldn't pull over there, it was full of cars and trucks passing on the right. At least there were no scooters.

Just a few weeks prior I had been in Mainland China, Beijing and Shanghai specifically, working for the Aerospace, Ballistics and Ordinance Ministry (ABOM). They make rockets and missiles for China's space program and the military. Now I am in Taiwan and for some reason the Chinese government has decided to threaten Taiwan by launching missiles over this island nation just to prove that they can do it. People were quite nervous. We were sure China didn't mean to hit Taiwan, just frighten the citizens into giving up and joining China. Of course, the Taiwanese knew that their brethren on the Mainland were about as competent as they were, so there was no guarantee that something wouldn't go wrong (*broking*) and cause a missile to fall short and crash into Taiwan killing someone.

It was also campaign season, which no doubt was part of the reason the Chinese chose this time to test their missiles. One of the candidates for president who was very pro-independence took a fishing boat out to the area where the missiles were crashing into the sea and was videotaped by a news crew shaking his fist at the missiles. I felt somewhat responsible, having just helped the Chinese improve their missile technology in my work there. I emailed the rep in China and told him where I was and asked him to please tell the ABOM guys I had worked with to stop with the missile launching already. The local English language radio station, ICRT, which all the cab drivers tuned their radios to whenever I got in the cab had an interesting take on the whole thing. They would start the traffic report with, "And now for our missile report,... I mean traffic report." It was funny, but not that funny. I didn't like being in a war zone without a gun. The missiles even affected air travel. Planes between Hong Kong and Taiwan were being rerouted to avoid the missile flight zone. It was kind of scary!

Up in Hsinchu I got another really clean hotel, the Lakeshore. This place was near what was once a recreational lake that had since silted in and become more of a swamp. Nobody swims in Taiwan anyway, so no big loss. No matter, the hotel was very posh, complete with thick down comforters on the bed, an excellent bar and restaurant and very friendly staff. While drinking there one night I met some Germans who were there helping the Taiwanese at some chemical plant. Germans are to chemicals what Americans are to semiconductors. They were staying at some nearby condos, for six month assignments. I was horrified. Germans are extremely clean people and have a violent dislike of filth, and here they are living in one of the filthiest countries in the world. They survived the same way I did, by imbibing as much beer as possible, thereby killing any disease organisms that might get into their digestive tract.

The Proxsi guys liked to take me out to eat, and eventually they figured out that I liked beer, so they offered me Taiwan Beer. It was a damn good beer, a Pilsner originally brewed by a German, and they kept the recipe true to the original. One night a group of us, including the husbands of some of the gals who worked at Proxsi went out to dinner. There was much toasting, "Campai!" in my direction, and many odd creatures they called food. I noticed that some of the husbands where ganging up on me, five guys each taking a turn at getting me to drink a full glass of beer with a "Compai!" Only the person toasted and the toaster have to drink, so it was five against one. In other words I was drinking five times as much beer as everyone else. Eventually I got so full I had to do something about it. I went to the bathroom, or toilet and went into a stall. They only had the squat down kind of toilet, just a porcelain hole in the floor. I found it very easy to stand up and vomit straight into the hole in the floor and empty myself out so I could handle another hour of "Compai!" with these guys. They must have thought I had an infinite capacity to drink Taiwan Beer!

In Hsinchu I visited one customer after another. At one place they were working on a device test program that had a Digital to Analog

Convertor in it, my specialty. The program was for a Japanese customer, and two of the customer representatives were there to make sure the Taiwanese could test their part. The test program wasn't working right and I was helping while the Japanese guys hung out, ready to give up and go home. I got the analog part working but they were still having trouble with the last remaining digital test. This was not my forte, but I looked at it and said, "I know what it is!" They missed one little directive and because I had been doing the training on this machine, I knew what it was. We tweaked the program and it worked like a champ. The engineers where ecstatic, the Japanese customers were pleased and the manager was so happy he invited me out to dinner to celebrate. When we got there, *I* was placed in the seat of honor, opposite the door rather than the Japanese customers. We ate and drank like there was no tomorrow. Hey, I was in Taiwan with Chinese missiles flying over my head, maybe there wouldn't be a tomorrow.

One dish that takes some getting used to is lobster sashimi. They take a live Rock Lobster, rip his tail off him, stuff the stump of his abdomen onto a plate heaped with ice and scatter his tail meat around his now slowly dying carcass. The "blood" from this ordeal is captured into a small pitcher and mixed with wine. Now you pick up a piece of raw lobster tail with your chopsticks, wave it in front of the poor dying lobster and say something rude about eating him alive and then eat the meat. Of course being the white guy, it was my honor to drink the lobster blood. After a few rounds I noticed it wasn't anyone else's honor to drink it, just mine.

This became a common theme in Taiwan, a game of *let's see what we can get this white guy to eat!* It might have been meant in good fun so I took it that way. Whenever I was asked to help pick from the menagerie of dead animals for our dinner, I usually picked the ugliest most disgusting looking thing, because I knew if I didn't, they would just pick them for me without my permission anyway. I could always sterilize it with plenty of Taiwan Beer.

After this huge dinner, with many *Compais* to me and my brilliant mind that saved the day, it was time to go. As we parted ways in front of the restaurant the manager said you to me, "You are a very good drinker, you almost drink better than Heath Kitt!" That meant a lot to me. Earlier in my career I met Mr. Kitt personally when he was president of Steppenwolf. I have an autographed copy of his book, he is an icon, a world traveler and tester guy who is a legend in Taiwan and around the world. Quite a complement indeed!

The next day I visited another customer who used our testers, Spilware. Great name for a company that deals with electronics and chemicals. I had done some work for Spilware before. I had installed and integrated a new 8 inch wafer prober that I was trained on in the States.

Spilware was about to move a device with three integrated Digital to Analog convertors onto one of our testers. It was a triple RAMDAC, a new kind of device for generating the Red, Green and Blue (RGB) signals to drive a computer video monitor. They wanted this RAMDAC tested on their new Steppenwolf testers and moved off their older Tritium testers. I gave them a short class on the basics, feeling very smug with my success the day before. The engineers seemed to understand and were ready to tackle the device, or so I thought. I got back to the States with an aura of success beaming like a halo around me. I drank as well as Heath Kitt *and* I solved many problems and was loved and adored by my customers. Soon, very soon I would be brought back to reality.

Little did I know that while I was on the plane home, Proxsi decided that it would be best for me to come back to Taiwan and help Spilware develop the analog portion of the test program for the RAMDAC. Won had mostly finished the digital portion of the test program and the Spilware engineers were so impressed with my lecture that they decided I was the man for the job. Oh great, home two days and now I have to go back to Taiwan, after being there two weeks. I negotiated with my boss and arranged to go there for a week, leaving on Friday. I could always extend my stay if I needed to, but I figured that would be enough. Again I was being too optimistic. Of course if I was any less optimistic, I would have never set foot on the plane!

Leaving Friday afternoon put me there Saturday night thanks to the International Date Line. Another precious weekend gone. I couldn't find my cab driver (or he couldn't find me) and so after a while I gave up and hired a guy who said he could take me to Hsinchu. I gave him a faxed copy of a business card for the hotel I was supposed to be going to, The Candy. Asians have a strange way of naming things. I always got a kick out of the scooter names, like Fuzzy. "Only real men ride a Fuzzy!" Who does their marketing?

We had a pleasant chat on the trip to Hsinchu and he gave me his business card and told me he could take me anywhere in Taiwan I wanted to go. His specialty was the CKS airport to Hsinchu run, but he would do anything I wanted. I thought it would be a good idea to keep this guy's card. I might be able to use a Taiwanese taxi driver who was loyal to me and not to Proxsi.

We arrived in Hsinchu and he dropped me off and drove away while I went inside. Except that it wasn't The Candy, it was a hotel owned by the same company, The Comfort Business Center. The receptionist called The Candy and found that I did have a reservation there, but not here. She said I could take a cab there, or they could give me a room here. A bit weary from the trip I told them I would stay here, why go across town to The Candy. Why indeed?

The Comfort Business Center, The Candy and the world famous bar Mr. Seven were all owned by the same guy. The girls who worked at these places worked all of them. On more than one occasion I would come down in the morning to find the receptionist serving breakfast severely hung over from a long night of drinking and cavorting with customers at Mr. Seven. It was hilarious! They would sometimes relate their stories to me over breakfast. Nothing like a prostitute confessional over breakfast to start your day.

The Comfort Business Center certainly wasn't the Grand Hai Lai, Hsinchu still didn't yet have a decent hotel, this was the best they could do. It had some issues. It did have the fancy window escape ladder to get down to the street past the plastic coated electrical power lines. It also seemed to have a leak at the joint between the wall and the floor. One night when it was raining cats and dogs, I got up in the middle of the night to pass some of the Taiwan Beer my kidneys had finished processing and noticed that the floor was soaking wet. Had I gotten up and pissed on the floor in my sleep? Nope, just a leaky wall, nothing to worry about. I looked out the window and saw a woman washing dishes in the rain outside. She was one of the thousands of street vendors serving food from a sidewalk stand. She had a tub of dishes that she was washing in the gutter. Rainwater was rushing down the street, pouring into her tub so she could rinse the dishes. I thought about how many times I had watched Taiwanese men spit on the street, now the rain was washing all that and more into the gutter to help this lady rinse her dishes. *Oh My God*, I was right about these folks all along. Can there possibly be enough Taiwan Beer in the world to keep me alive?

After re-arriving in Taiwan, since I had been there only a few days ago I got a decent nights sleep. I seldom get jet lagged going east to west, only the other way around and only a week earlier I had been in this time zone, so readjusting wasn't too much of an issue.

It was now Sunday morning. Won came to pick me up, and off we went into Spilware to get started on the program. I started work on the pattern and in just an hour had it written and ready to go using a very sneaky trick that very few people at the time could have known about. The pattern I was given came from a Japanese tester that had an APG, an Algorithmic Pattern Generator, which I was familiar with from my days at RadChek and from reading Heath Kitt's book on automated test. The Steppenwolf tester I was coding for didn't have an APG, but I understood what the APG was doing. It would have generated a pattern of 0, 1, 2, 3, 4, 5,...all the way up to 255 to create a kind of staircase signal that we would capture with the mixed signal hardware. Think about testing a staircase to make sure every step is safe to use. You would march up the staircase and if one of the steps was bad, you would fall through and die. This was quite likely in Taiwan.

To duplicate the pattern I used a fancy version of copy and paste so that I could replicate the incrementing pattern in just a few minutes. I was quite sharp for a guy working on a Sunday who had gotten off a plane just ten hours earlier after flying all the way across the Pacific Ocean.

We ran the program and looked at the output of the chip and sure enough, it was putting out the right signal. Holy crap, I could be done by Monday! I wasn't really surprised because I experienced this kind of success with the other customer who had wined a dined me only a week earlier for doing almost exactly the same job. The next day, Monday, I met the manager and the test engineer, a Taiwanese fellow named Neeto. Neeto had gotten his BSEE degree in the U.S. and so knew a lot about the States. However Neeto wasn't really much of a programmer, which was why Won and I were working on this program for him. Left to his own devices he couldn't code his way out of a wet paper bag, but he didn't have to, he was the customer.

I took on the frightening task of soldering coax cable to the existing probe card as this test was to be done at wafer sort. There was a huge risk that I would damage the extremely delicate probe needles by doing this modification, but as it turned out, everything was fine. The modification worked perfectly and the customer was happy with our progress.

The next day, we started probing a whole wafer and noticed that something strange was happening. After ten to twenty devices had been tested, the yield went from ninety percent to under fifty percent. How could the yield go down like that? Besides, when we went back and probed devices that had already passed, they now failed. I asked Neeto about this behavior. Did they see the same thing on the Tritium? The answer was no, same wafers, same tests, the yield on the Tritium tester was consistently ninety percent. The customer said it had to be **my** test program. Of course I wondered how it had suddenly became *my* test program when I had only arrived a few days earlier. Besides, it wasn't just the tests that I had coded.

Other tests were failing too! How could it be that adding a single test caused other portions of the test program to fail? The customer was adamant, it was Steppenwolf's fault, that means it's **my** fault and they wanted it fixed immediately.

I looked at everything, I questioned every addition I had made to the program. We went back and ran the original program and found that it had the same problem. It had to be their wafers, we protested! "No, this is not possible, it must be your tester!" The evidence was on our side, but they wouldn't listen, they said that they had the same wafers running on the Tritium and didn't have this problem. As it turned out, this was a lie, but we wouldn't find out for another three months.

I spent the next two and a half weeks killing myself trying to make this program work and observing the quirks of the Taiwanese. For example, on the test floor at Spilware they played music for the operators, but since the testers and handlers and various other machines were so loud, they had to really crank it up. It was nearly impossible to think with this booming Asian rock music playing over the din of the machines banging, whirring and clanking away. I resorted to wearing earplugs all the time.

Another incident that made me doubt the supposed superior reasoning abilities of the Taiwanese was the failure of Won's car to start. Going out to lunch one day, Won could not get his car started. It just wouldn't crank. He thought his battery was dead and made the "come hither" sign with his index finger, which means **death** in Chinese culture. Never use the come hither sign to ask a Chinese person to come to you, it's taken as "I want to kill you." Probably not what you intended.

While Wan tried to start his car I noticed that the dome light inside didn't dim when he turned the key, which meant there was nothing wrong with the battery. I explained the point and told him to turn on the headlights and try cranking the engine while I observed their brightness. Not only were the headlights plenty bright, even in daylight, when he turned the key the headlights remained at exactly the same brightness, meaning the starter was not engaging, and was not drawing down the battery voltage. Won, who had a Masters degree in Computer Science should have understood the meaning of my tests but he didn't believe me, so he went off to ask the guard at Spilware for a jump. If he wasn't taking his lunchtime nap that is. All Taiwanese employees take a nap at lunchtime, even the security guards. In the U.S. Navy, they court-martial you for sleeping on watch but in Taiwan it's just part of the culture.

So here comes Won with the guard in tow. While he was gone I noticed that he had not put the shifter fully into Park. It was the Park/Shift lockout switch. As they approached I moved the shifter a touch, turned the key and it fired right up. I couldn't help but question the intelligence of the Taiwanese when a guy with a Masters degree misses something so simple with so many obvious indicators that it wasn't the battery. This is endemic, a symptom of a people who can't do simple troubleshooting, no matter how much schooling they have. It meant I had job security, but it also meant that I had to fight them tooth and nail to listen to my advice and most likely they would just ignore it.

Day after day, week after week, killing myself for twelve to fourteen hours a day, eating the most horrendous things, living the in the Comfort Business Center, I was becoming increasingly disgusted with Taiwan.

Proxsi noticed my rapidly declining state of mind, and ordered Won to take especially good care of me. Won took to me every fancy place he could think of for dinner, I ate everything from live fish to duck tongues to bunny rabbit ears and drank an ocean of Taiwan Beer. I spent my days either coding or rerunning a wafer while occasionally retiring to my only escape from the test floor, the roof of Spilware. Since I didn't have an office, I had few places I could go to get away from the incessant noise that the Taiwanese seemed determined to make, and the roof was the one place nobody ever went. From the roof I could see a huge building across the street. It was TSHMUK, a major semiconductor fab in Taiwan. I wondered if Spilware **got its wafers from them**.

I have now been in Taiwan for almost five of the last six weeks and we are coming up on Memorial Day weekend in the States. I had already made plans to go on a big camping trip with my family and the neighbors to a lake in Oregon, and I had the only boat. If I can't get out of Taiwan, I blow a three day weekend for two families. I gotta get out of here!

As we approached my planned departure date, my boss's boss, Flim Flamman arrived to check on my progress. I explained the situation and he was sympathetic to my plight, but there was nothing he could do. The customer was certain that I was an incompetent boob and they would punish me by keeping me there until I solved the problem. No matter what I did it became clearer and clearer to me that it was *their* problem and not mine, but I couldn't prove it.

Flim must have gotten in touch with my boss Fran, because the next thing I know, my old buddy, Red Stevens, arrived at Spilware. He had been en-route to Kaohsiung to deal with some other issue, but Fran diverted him to

Hsinchu to help me out. Red brought with him a special program that might reveal the problem, but it turned out to be as worthless as everything else we tied. Lucky Red also got stuck in the Comfort Business Center, he had been planning on going to the Grand Hai Lai in Kaohsiung so it was a bit of a shock.

Then on Thursday evening, the night before I was scheduled to leave for home, Mei Way and a troop of Proxiites joined me at Spilware to take me out to dinner to persuade me to stay. My good friend Ho Lee Hung was there too. Proxsi was pulling out all the stops to persuade me to stay. I was just about to start another round of probing to see if any of my latest changes fixed the problem and the **Goddamn prober crapped out**! I watched as the Spilware technician tried to figure out what went wrong, and it was like watching a replay of Won and his balky car. The guy had no idea how to troubleshoot the problem, he did the Chinese equivalent of *ennee meeny miney moe*, and decided to change out the power supply with no evidence that the power supply was in any way at fault. I couldn't believe it, my fate was now tied to a whole building of incompetent boobs who were calling me incompetent.

We went to dinner, me in total depression and disgust. Mei pleaded with me to stay, every time I said no, he ordered more beer. He thought he could buy my servitude with Taiwan Beer. He was very polite but continued to beg me to stay. When dinner was over they took me back to my hotel and left Ho Lee to persuade me not to leave.

Ho Lee and I had been friends for a long time, but I was plain with him, his continued haranguing would not work. I would not stay. I understood that his job was to persuade me to stay, but he wouldn't change my mind. Ho Lee finally left me alone in my room, realizing he couldn't stay there all night. I set my plan into action. I called Fran and filled him in. I told him I was going to leave or quit my job. He said of course I should leave, Red would take over for me.

I went through my briefcase and found the business card of the taxi driver who had brought me to Hsinchu from CKS airport. I called him, and despite the fact it was nearly midnight he answered. I explained my plan. Won would arrive at 9AM to pick me up, I wanted the driver to pick me up at 8AM **sharp**. I also made him swear to me that he would not contact my employer and alert them I was leaving. I got him to agree that *I* was his customer, *I* would be paying him, and he was beholden to **me**, not Proxsi.

The next morning I packed up and went to Red Stevens' room. I knocked on the door and after a minute he answered the door in his underwear. He took one look at me standing there with my suitcase and said, "You fucker, you're leaving me here, aren't you?" I told him about my conversation with Fran. He would confirm it of course but he wasn't happy about becoming the sacrificial lamb at Spilware.

I checked out of the hotel, and was ecstatic at seeing my taxi driver arrive to take me to the airport. I arrived at the airport at 10AM and it was way too early to check into my 5PM flight. I figured that Won had come to pick me up at the hotel and finding that I had checked out, he would drive to the airport to hunt me down. So now, I had to hide out in the airport for seven hours. A six foot tall white guy in an airport full of five foot tall Chinese people stands out like a sore thumb, I did not hold out much hope of evading even a cursory search by the Proxiites. However, once I checked into my flight, I would be safe. They couldn't come get me once I was past Immigration and Security. Could I hide out for *seven hours*? I knew my biggest mistake would be to hang out at the Burger King. Still, I couldn't resist grabbing a Whopper for lunch. I'd eaten nothing but unrecognizable sea creatures, crab roe, raw lobster and duck tongues for weeks, I couldn't pass up a chance to get a decent burger. I started to think I shouldn't be so paranoid. The hours were passing and still, no sign of Won. *I was going to make it!* I got in line to check into my flight. I felt like the guy swimming in the water after a ship wreck, watching the sharks circling while the rescue helicopter lowers a sling to pluck me from the water.

When I got to the head of the line it was like the helicopter exploded and fell out of the sky. *"I'm sorry Mister Bullard, we cannot allow you to check in. Your friend So Ree Jack is on his way to speak to you."* Un-fucking-believable! Proxsi had called the airline and told them to not let me check in, and So Ree was coming to the airport to drag me back to Hsinchu to that nasty test floor, to that building full of incompetent boobs, and quite probably to a lifetime of living at the Comfort Business Center.

I tried to contemplate my options. I could go to another airline and get a flight out, but if my boss disagreed with that strategy I would be stuck paying for a two thousand dollar plane ticket out of my own pocket, and not have a job to boot. I decided to wait for So Ree and deal with him directly. We were old friends after all, he owed me a lot. I hoped that would be enough.

When So Ree arrived, he took me to the airline's Business Class Lounge and proceeded to fill me with Taiwan Beer. I made my case: if he tried to stop me from leaving Taiwan I would instantly quit. Furthermore, I had permission from Fran to leave Taiwan and Proxsi was not my boss. So

Ree finally relented. He took me back to the ticket counter where he told the agent to go ahead and let me check in. I got my boarding pass, and So Ree walked me to Immigration. We said goodbye, I was going home.

Leaving Asia on Friday gets you home on Friday. The wife had us all packed up to go camping, so off we went, me delirious with happiness and jet lag, or so I thought. We made it to the lake, tried some water skiing in the frigid water and truly enjoyed life. Saturday night sleeping in the tent I broke out in a sweat while still freezing. I was sick, *really sick*. I was so sick I decided I had better drive home leaving the kids and the wife to finish out the camping trip with the neighbors. I drove the Astro home towing our ski boat behind me, so sick with fever I thought I would pass out. Finally at home, I went to bed and didn't get up for four days.

It turns out Neeto had caught SARS, Severe Acute Respiratory Syndrome and given it to me just before I left Taiwan. SARS was a big deal in Asia while I was traveling there. All the airports had infrared fever monitors at all the arriving gates and customs areas to scan for people infected with SARS. If you walked through these areas with a fever the guards would take you into custody and put you in isolation.

Red later told me Neeto spent a week in the hospital, I recovered in my own bed. The Taiwanese had damn near killed me! Had I not left when I did, I would have ended up in a Taiwanese hospital, and given the state of intellect I had seen there, I might have died there. Taiwan is another place I would not want to die. *Next up on the menu, Bai Yuan Gong (white ape man) sashimi!*

Three weeks later, Red Stevens came back. They still hadn't figured out the problem. Red posited that it could be some kind of contamination on the wafers that was coating the probe needles and causing the problem. He also knew a guy who worked at a company that could confirm it. Spilware shipped some of the wafers to Red so he could get them checked out. When they arrived, all but one of the wafers was *broking*. Spilware had done such a poor job of packing them, they crumbled into shards in their container.

A few weeks later Red gave me the news, there **had** been contamination on the wafers that came from TSHMUK, yes, the place across the street that I viewed from the rooftop of Spilware. The contamination was being picked up by the probe needles and increased the resistance of the contact to the chips. How could this be true? Hadn't Spilware sworn that the Tritium testers were successfully testing the very same wafers? Then came the word from Taiwan. They had lied to us, **we** were testing a **new lot** of wafers using a new process. Once those new wafers got to the Tritiums they saw the very same symptoms. It never was my fault, the customer had spent *six weeks* lying to us and kept Red and myself hostage for nearly a month each, not to mention nearly killing me with a nasty case of SARS.

On a later trip I confronted Won about this, he simply told me "We don't talk about this anymore." Good idea, can't handle the truth huh? *You bastards!* You incompetent *lying bastards!* They had nearly killed me with their lies!

I eventually left Steppenwolf, partly due to this debacle, but came back later as a Marketing Applications Engineer. In this job I didn't have to write test programs, I merely had to go to customer sites, give PowerPoint presentations, look over data sheets and recommend options to the customers. I went to Taiwan again and spoke to customers, but it was such a different role that it really didn't bother me. I had eaten everything they had thrown at me. That is, except on this trip when they tried to get me to eat the fermented tofu, chòu dòufu which smells exactly like shit. Since I had proven myself in the past, Proxsi let me off the hook. There is a logic in learning to eat things that smell that bad. You won't starve to death just because the food choices are unpalatable.

When I joined TestEz I also had to travel to Taiwan, by now I was an old pro. I was an expert at getting around in Taiwan. I **flew** between Taipei and Kaohsiung instead of riding in a car with my friend Won. Won wasn't my rep anyway, TestEz used a different company, called Heman, which was also based in Hsinchu.

One day while in Hsinchu, I visited the Heman offices and noticed that they occupied the first few floors of a building that looked very familiar. I checked the legend and found that it was the same building that Proxsi was in! I took the elevator up to the seventh floor and went in. I told the receptionist I wanted to speak with Won, and there he was! My old friend. He showed me around, even gave me a tour of their first floor demo test facility. In previous years it had been a Hot Pot restaurant. A Hot Pot is a small charcoal fired grill with a boiling pot of broth in the middle. The waitress brings you various meats and things and you boil them or roast them yourself in the pot and grill. Proxsi had moved their testers into this portion of the building as both a development lab and a working test floor.

My other job on this trip was going to Semicon Taiwan. I had to give demonstrations of my voice activated program that I had shown at Semicon West in San Francisco. The problem was it didn't work very well in Taiwan because of the vastly higher noise level. The show was very well attended, the building wasn't adequately cooled, and the noise level was extreme, to the point where my demo hardly worked at all. Lam Thong, the Asia salesman was with me on this trip, he turned out to be a good guy too. Since he was raised in the States, at least he understood what being an American was all about. As kind as the Taiwanese guys were, they didn't quite get the independent freedom thing.

One night Lam and our Heman rep, Lucky Lin went out on the town for some fun. You must always be suspicious when a Taiwanese guy wants to have fun, especially a guy named Lucky. We went to a bar and once we got inside, three girls met us and sat down with us at a table. *Oh Christ* I thought, I know what this is about! I had had an experience like this in Shanghai, China. I know the drill here.

I tried a bit of conversation. One of the girls asked me my sign, gee, she must be very deep, I thought. I tried making it interesting, explaining to her how the Zodiac worked, etcetera, but she wasn't interested in astrology or astronomy. It was obvious she wanted to extract my money from me through my penis.

"Where is the toilet?" I asked, they pointed. *Damn, the opposite direction of the front door!* I went to the bathroom, spent a minute there, then headed back in the direction of the table and just kept on going as I said, "*See ya!*"

I went downstairs walking as fast as I could, got a few blocks away and hailed a cab. I had grabbed the hotel business card earlier when I left to go out on the town, so I had a way to get there even though I didn't know the name of the hotel I was staying at. Just give the card to the taxi driver and he will take me there. That was quite clever I thought to myself. When I got back to the room I had a message on my phone. It was Lam. I called him back and he asked why I left. I told him, I don't screw around with girls who aren't my wife. He said he was worried about me. I told him "Lam, I've been coming to Taiwan longer that you have, you don't have to worry about me in Taiwan, I promise you that." After all I had been through, this was no sweat!

The next day I talked to Lam about his experience with the girls. It seems he ended up playing a game where you try to steal a strawberry from the lips of the girl and they end up kissing the strawberry with your lips just millimeters from theirs. Lam, being married admitted that it was a stupid thing to do and wished he had come with me rather than hang out with these girls. He kept saying, "What was I *thinking?*" It wasn't what he was thinking, it was what he was drinking.

While at Heman I taught a class on mixed signal. These guys were like fresh Proxsi guys, no idea of what mixed signal was and since we only had two days they weren't going to have a very good idea of what it was even after the class. At least they had some exposure.

To thank us and his other vendors for attending Semicon Taiwan, the president of Heman threw a big party which I attended. They had plenty of beer and wine and good food at last, it was a quite a party.

At the show I gave a demo for a guy from a company called TestRite, a little test house in Hsinchu and this guy became very interested in the TestEz system. A month or so after I got back to the States, Lam Thong asked me if I could go back to Taiwan to talk to TestRite and some other customers. I said fine, no problem and made the arrangements. I got a flight to Taiwan by way of San Francisco, with a layover in Hong Kong and finally to Taipei. I had to fly from Portland to SFO first.

When I got on the 747 in San Francisco, it turned out that they had an electrical problem in my section of coach. The reading lights didn't work, nor did the audio for the movies they would be showing. They wouldn't let you open the window shade and let the sunlight in. Even though we were chasing the Sun across the Pacific, they tried to keep the cabin dark for the movie. We were supposed to just sit in the dark and stare into space for fourteen hours. Luckily I had planned for just such an eventuality. I had just bought a portable DVD player with three **extra** batteries and about twenty movies. So while my seat mates sat in the dark for fourteen hours, I watched movie after movie after movie. I recharged my batteries in Hong Kong and then watched one more movie en route to CKS airport.

After making my way to Hsinchu I got a room at the brand new Ambassador Hotel, a top notch five star hotel. The Heman guy came to pick me up and took me to TestRite. I recognized the head engineer right way, and he recognized me. I had been here before working on some such problem and I apparently did right by them, because the engineer was very happy to see me. We discussed the device he wanted to test, it was a WiFi codec that they had been trying to test on an old Steppenwolf product. Basically it is the chip that does all the work on your WiFi connection, either in your phone, computer or internet box. When he showed me what he had been doing I realized right away that our little TestEz machine could test it, and do a much better job than the Steppenwolf box. We went to lunch at a nearby place and wrapped up the deal.

Back in the States it was time for another party, the annual TestEz sales meeting held in Manteca, California, which in some ways is similar to Taiwan. During the meeting, I gave a presentation on the mixed signal business we had done: virtually none, but I did find a nice slide that got some laughs. Google Sofa King, where prices are Sofa King low. I thought Mick was going to have a heart attack when he finally got it. However, the sales people were intrigued by the TestRite deal. After my presentation the CEO, Bob Hood told me, "Dan, I want you to do everything you can to get this business, I want this account." I promised I would get it for him.

Then suddenly TestRite got cold feet. They saw a specification in our tester that they couldn't reconcile with their chip's test needs. I tried to convince them through email that it would be all right, but they couldn't understand. I arranged to fly to Taiwan again with Lam Thong. We had a meeting with TestRite and I taught them a mini-class on Aliasing, a technique that I was an expert on. Most of the world was, and still is totally uneasy with aliasing. MIT has a video in their on-line curriculum that says that Aliasing is bad. No wonder these guys were scared. After a two hour mini-seminar on Aliasing, Dan's Rules and the new Bullard-Reynolds Frequency Measure Technique they agreed that it would work for them, so they signed the purchase order. We had our first order, and the order that Bob, the CEO of TestEz had told me to get.

I flew back home very pleased with myself. I had spent two full days on a plane to attend a two hour meeting and lunch with a customer, but it had resulted in an order that saved our tester from being canned by the CEO.

The TestEz Philippines office assigned an applications engineer to the TestRite project, a fellow named Chris Weemaway. I had previously trained Chris on the tester and he had experience with mixed signal so I figured he could handle it. Now he had to get the information from TestRite and start work on the project. It was a big, big project. Over the next few months Chris made good progress, but some tests he just couldn't get working right. As he got ready to fly to Taiwan to deliver the project, I told him I was worried about him going over there without the program working, but he assured me he could handle it. I happened to be in San Jose for almost a month getting ready for the upcoming Semicon West show in San Francisco and offered to help him several times a day, but he would have none of it. He would finish the program in Taiwan.

Chris got to Taiwan and was still having trouble getting one group of tests working. Lam asked me to fly over and help him out. It was Semicon Taiwan time again, and I was having trouble getting a room at the Ambassador Hotel because of all the visitors, even though the Ambassador was in Hsinchu and the show was in Taipei. My flight would put me in Taiwan on Sunday, but the Ambassador couldn't give me a room till Monday night. So I booked a room at another Ambassador hotel in Taipei for Sunday night.

When I got to the Ambassador in Taipei I arranged a taxi to Hsinchu for the next day. I was getting really good at this international travel gig. Because I was staying in Taipei, the Heman people were going crazy trying to figure out where I was. I explained to them I had it under control, I was a real *road warrior* by now, I didn't need much hand holding, especially in Taiwan. For the record, the Ambassador in Taipei was fantastic.

Most of Taipei is actually quite nice and modern. However, I do remember a visit to Snake Alley which somewhat dissolved the illusion of civilization. All up and down the street vendors kill live snakes, drain their blood, cook the meat and mix the blood with other ingredients to make various disgusting dishes. I was there with So Ree Jack who kept hounding me to eat something. I let him order me a cob of corn roasted on an outdoor vendor's BBQ cart, which I thought would be safe enough. That is, until the vendor started brushing some kind of sauce on my otherwise pristine and relatively sterile cob of corn. Oh, well, at least there was a 7-11 nearby so I could buy a bottle of Taiwan Beer. While eating our street-side meal, a garbage truck pulled up just a foot away and loaded up all the vendor garbage collected over the week. So lovely to be eating a meal next to tons of week old garbage.

I made it to the Ambassador in Hsinchu the next day and then got a real shock. Despite having reservation for the whole week, the registrar informed me they could only put me up for two nights. I would be homeless on Wednesday. Suddenly images of the Comfort Business Center flooded back. There was only one good hotel in Hsinchu and they didn't have room for me. I went back to my room and made plans to leave Taiwan on Wednesday, I would not stay here if I couldn't stay in the Ambassador.

Then I got a phone call from my boss, Mick Archangel. He was at Semicon Taiwan and was quite upset that I would ditch the customer after two days. I told him I was not going to stay anywhere but the Ambassador. He informed me that Heman had gotten the hotel to give me a room through Saturday. I told him that I had already arranged to fly home on Wednesday. He ordered me to change it, fly First Class if you have to, but don't leave before Saturday. Fine, I guess that's good enough. What I found amusing is that while on the phone, Mick complained that he had never felt so uncomfortable in his life. The air at Semicon Taiwan was hot, humid, dirty and stinky. The noise level at the show was driving him crazy and the food choices were disgusting. This was his first trip to Taiwan and he's ordering me to stay here? "*Welcome to the party pal*" as Bruce Willis playing the role of John McClane in *Die Hard* put it.

Again I was in Taiwan working on the test floor, which I was really sick of, and as a Marketing Engineer, I shouldn't have been doing, but Chris needed help. I only wish he had let me help him in San Jose!

Chris seemed to fight me on every suggestion, just as he had when I tried to help him in San Jose months earlier. I couldn't seem to persuade him to let me "have the reins" and drive the debug effort. After a week of fighting with it we had really made no progress. In a Friday afternoon meeting with the TestEz VP of Sales in the room, the TestRite people asked me if the tester could really do what I had said it could. I said yes, it could. The TestRite head engineer said, "I trust you." With that they let me go and let Chris continue to work on the problem.

A couple of weeks later, Chris was tiring of being in Taiwan and needed to go home to the Philippines and take care of a few things. This was my chance: I would fly to Taiwan and work on the program without Chris there, since all he did was thwart all my attempts at debugging. I got a room at the Ambassador, flew in and got to work on the program. One of the Heman guys accompanied me there every day.

The Ambassador Hotel was a big step up from the Comfort Business Center, but it was not up to the standard of most U.S. hotels. The hotel was a very tall "atrium style" hotel, rather like an Embassy Suites, but much, much taller, which meant that the open atrium extended some 40 floors. One day I took the elevator down to breakfast and found some of the dining tables taped off and there seemed to be a ton of glass on the floor. A glass panel from the twenty-second floor had slipped out of its mounts and fallen twenty-two stories to crash into the lobby level dining area. Had anyone been sitting there? Had anyone been injured by flying glass? I couldn't get an answer but this is just the kind of thing one can expect when in a third world country. Life is cheap, and if you value your life you shouldn't take the risk.

Another day, a typhoon moved into the area and knocked out the power to the hotel and surrounding areas. From the thirty-fourth floor I could watch transformers down on the street level burst into balls of fire and sparks as the storm slapped power lines together. The hotel staff was all on leave during this time, so I sat in my room with no power, watching the mayhem unfold hoping that the skyscraper I was in wouldn't collapse in the wind. The hotel offered one meal a day because that's all the cook and wait staff could muster.

Once all the pandemonium was over, I got back to work at TestRite. In three days I solved three major problems, and at last had results that looked right to the TestRite people. The TestRite guys were very impressed, but now the issue was test time. It was taking our tester over ten seconds to test the part, but the competitor's tester was taking only two and half seconds. Chris had filled the program with tons of extra stuff to help him solve the problems he was fighting and that extra code was slowing us down, but this didn't account for all the extra time. He was also using a technique called averaging to cheat, which I thought was a terrible thing to do to a company named TestRite. I was going to have to take the program back to the States to get the speed up. TestRite agreed that would be OK.

While at the Ambassador I ran into a friend of mine from my earliest days in the business, Ken Thomas. Ken was one of the better software engineers at RadChek and we also worked together at Steppenwolf. Ken and I went to the nearby Pig and Whistle, an English style pub with decent food including burgers and French fries. Hsinchu was looking better all the time, good hotel, good food and good friends. A week here was bearable, more than that is too much for me.

Back in San Jose, Red Stevens and I worked on the program together. I had brought him to TestEz to help me and he was invaluable. We quickly cleaned up Chris' program but found that most of the sloth was not due to Chris' coding. It was in the system code. TestRite had told us to try using a faster PC for the system computer, blaming the sloth on the DSP statements, but I knew that wasn't the problem. Malcolm Reynolds had coded all the DSP and I already knew it was *lightning fast*. We finally convinced engineering that the digital system software was slowing us down and so they started working on it.

However there were still some problems to solve and I told Mick I couldn't just live in San Jose until I got it all figured out. To allow me to stay home more, the company sent a tester up to Portland so I could work on the program at my own pace and in my hometown. It cost them a fortune to upgrade the electrical service in our office to accommodate this machine, not to mention building the machine itself, but I couldn't live in San Jose until this customer was happy, it could take months.

TestRite was getting nervous. It was coming up on a year since they bought the tester and they still didn't have a working test program. I was having trouble getting the program to be robust. The timing values had to be tweaked for every different tester it ran on, which shouldn't have been the case. Auto-calibration is supposed to compensate for differences between testers. No one could figure it out. Eventually TestRite reneged on the deal to buy four testers and wanted TestEz to take back the one they had bought. Engineering had fixed many of the choke points in their system code that was making the tester run slow, but it just wasn't fast enough yet, or reliable enough for production. I was devastated.

Months later Bob, the CEO of TestEz came up to Portland for a visit. We had a new customer who had a need to test devices overseas, and I thought of TestRite. They still had their tester, but weren't using it for anything so maybe we could reconfigure TestRite's tester to test the new customer's device! I told Bob of my idea, he told me to my face "Fuck TestRite!" This certainly was a departure from the last sales meeting in Manteca where he **ordered me** to get their business.

Several months passed, then Malcolm Reynolds noticed a problem with the tester. In the configuration that TestRite had, the tester was not properly calibrated. The timing edges were all over the place, which could explain the trouble that Chris and I had seen in Taiwan. At first engineering blamed it on the changes I had requested to speed up the TestRite program, but after they backed out all those changes, the problem remained.

Then they found it: The software architect had botched the software so that tester **couldn't be calibrated**, no matter what. Everything Chris and I had gone through, the two days of flying for a two hour meeting, the weeks in Taiwan, Chris' months and months away from his family were doomed from the beginning because this guy hard coded one number into the software that should have been a variable. This and the fact that the very same guy had mangled the code so badly that the tester was slower than any other tester on the market. While it was great to finally be vindicated, the victory wasn't very sweet. Engineering grudgingly accepted blame, but wouldn't admit it to the customer, despite my pleas that they fly to Taiwan and accept the blame in front of TestRite. I even volunteered to fly to Taiwan and explain it to TestRite and apologize for the company, even though I was totally blameless. It had been my perseverance that had uncovered all the problems with the tester, but no one wanted me to do that.

So, after almost twenty trips to Taiwan to save the day time after time, making a good name for myself, good enough that TestRite was willing to buy a tester from me because of my reputation, my reputation in Taiwan was now destroyed. My name was dirt. All that work, all those flights, all those nights in crappy hotels eating both live and dead animals I never knew existed. All that Taiwan Beer. All that draught, for naught.

Gart: *I know where I'd like to be.*
Janie: *Where's that?*
Gart: *A place called Willoughby. A little town I manufactured in a dream.*
Janie: *Tell me about your dream Gart.*
Gart: *It was an odd dream, very odd dream. Willoughby. It was summer, very warm. Kids were barefooted, one of them had a fishing pole. It all looked like a Currier and Ives painting. Bandstand, bicycles, wagons. I've never seen such serenity. It's the way people must have lived a hundred years ago. Crazy dream....A place, a time where a man can live his life full measure. That's what he said, that's what that conductor said, a place where a man can live his life full measure.*
The Twilight Zone, A Stop At Willoughby by Rod Serling

Korea

"Bulgogi? Kamsahamnida! "

Thank you for the marinated beef (I hope it's not dog) in Korean

My first trip to South Korea was an unplanned side trip after a visit to Taiwan. I had been in Taiwan giving a training class and our Technical Sales Specialist (TSS) for Asia and old friend, So Ree Jack visited me. While out on the town drinking he told me I needed to go to Korea as he had just closed a deal there and the company, ElectroKook (Kook is Korean for "people") wanted me to look at some of their chips to explain how they might test them with the SOS3000 testers they had just bought. He told me it was a one day trip, go there, visit, have a meeting, have lunch, and then I could go home. Nothing to it. As usual So Ree was understating the depth of the assignment, but I wouldn't know that for another few days.

I wrapped up the class in Taiwan, got a flight to Korea and So Ree and I headed for the airport. While there I headed for a currency exchange kiosk to exchange my Taiwan dollars to Korean won. So Ree said don't bother, I could do that in Korea and we needed to get to our respective planes. So Ree was always late, or at least it seemed that way.

So I fly into Korea, about a two hour flight from Taiwan and arrive at Kimpo, the Seoul airport around 5PM local time. Now I need to exchange my money so I can get a cab to the hotel. Then I get some bad news: Korea and Taiwan don't have formal diplomatic relations, as Taiwan is no longer the official government of China. That's in Beijing now. Since they don't have formal ties, they don't exchange money either. The guy in the money exchange kiosk can't help me. The bank branch office at the airport is closed. Crap! Now I am in the Seoul airport with not one scrap of useful money, just a wad of useless Taiwan dollars. Taxis didn't take credit cards back then, I tried that. I was screwed.

I checked the outgoing flights, but at this hour of the day there was only one, headed for Guam. I could see me trying to explain to my boss how I ended up in Guam, skipping out on a new customer and trying to get reimbursed for that.

Eventually after about an hour, a man approached me offering a taxi ride. He was an unauthorized cab driver, which is illegal in Korea. I told him I only had Taiwan dollars, he said that was no problem. Finally, a solution! I wouldn't have to sleep in the airport!

So we got to his cab and I got inside. I asked him what he wanted for the ride, and he said he wanted the equivalent of $35 U.S.. That was kind of steep, but OK, fine. Then he said, no, hows about $50? Uh, OK... Then he said, no, how's about $70? Holy crap, this guy was really scaring me. I said, "OK, but that's it, no more!" He agreed and off we went. Now I was concerned, he could just pull over anywhere and demand more money, and my only choice was to pay it, or get out and walk, with no money and carry my big suitcase, assuming he would even let me have my suitcase. I was starting to dislike Korea. On the way I noticed a hotel bus going the same direction we were, on the side it said, "Seoul Hilton!" I was really tempted to tell him to drop me off, but figured I couldn't get the bus driver to stop for me anyway. People who have never left America can't imagine the constant danger Americans are in, not because of our foreign policy, or our "arrogance" but simply because we have money and the locals don't. That and the fact they don't have many scruples, as I was quickly finding out. We arrived at the hotel, quite a spectacular place, and I was very relieved, especially when he didn't demand more money to get my suitcase out of the trunk. For the record, he didn't get a tip.

At the hotel I had a message from our rep there, O.K. Dokie, a fellow I had trained on the SOS3000 a few months earlier. I called him back and told him about my predicament. He said there was no place I could exchange my Taiwan dollars, but he could lend me some money and I could repay him by smuggling some good cognac to him next time I visited. God, I was really starting to dislike Korea.

The next day O.K. picked me up at the hotel and off we went to ElectroKook. The place was drab and stark. I had to take my shoes off and wear some visitors sandals, tiny flip-flops really, worn by how many other people in the past? Everything was filthy. They had a shoehorn to help you change your shoes, but the handle was black with the years of accumulated skin oils and dirt. Oh God, I'm gonna catch something from this, I thought. I had to wear these tiny flip flops that ended about two inches from my heel which made walking difficult.

We started our meeting and the engineers at ElectroKook showed me some data sheets on the chips they wanted to test and asked me how long it would take me to write the programs. What? That's not what So Ree said I would be doing. Oh crap! He set me up! Now all of a sudden I had four chips to write programs for. The good news was that I would be allowed to do this in the States. The bad news was that in one week, one of the ElectroKook engineers, a Mr. Rhee would fly to Portland, Oregon and I was to get him an apartment, set him up with a rental car, train him and write the test programs for the four parts. Then I would come back to Korea and install and correlate the test programs I had written. My little side trip to Korea had turned into a nightmare assignment. I was going to have to talk to the boss about this one!

I had another problem — how to get back home. I had to fly out of Seoul back to Taipei's Chiang Kai-shek airport, then board my original flight leaving from Taiwan to...Korea, then onto the States from there. I called the airline and asked if I could just pick up the flight in Korea, they said no, if I wasn't on the plane, my seat was going to someone else. It just seemed silly to fly to Taiwan, only to fly back to Korea, then home. I called another airline that could fly me directly to Portland from Korea and they would take my ticket. I cancelled the other flight and was *so* happy to get back home.

When I got back to work at Steppenwolf I had to write up my explanation for why I spent $70 on a cab ride. My bosses boss, Flim Flamman explained that he understood, but that I could have just gotten a cab to take me to the hotel and they would pay for the cab out of my hotel bill. This is one of those Korea specific things that you would like to know before you go, but not something a neophyte would know. Oh well, lesson learned, and I did use that trick on a later trip.

Now I had to figure out where I was going to put this Korean guy. So instead of relaxing after an arduous Asia trip I had to scramble to find a furnished apartment with all the amenities, a rental car company that would rent to a Korean national, a place for him to shop, and grab a training room at Steppenwolf so I could train him, since there wasn't a scheduled class on this tester in the time frame we were looking at. I'm certain the Koreans assumed I would farm all this out to a group of subordinates, but I didn't have any, I was low man on the totem pole, I had to do all this myself. Don't forget, I still have four test programs to write while doing all of this including eight hours a day of teaching and trying to keep this guy entertained while he is in the States.

By the time Mr. Rhee arrived I had everything ready. He came with a rep from Steppenwolf Korea, a friendly fellow also named Mr. Rhee, another Korean. I got them into the apartment, took them to get the rental car, took them to the local Asian food store and got them moved in. It turned out that the Mr. Rhee who was our rep was going to be a virtual slave to Mr. Rhee, the customer from ElectroKook. I couldn't imagine that and even challenged him on this point. He said he was happy to do all the cooking, cleaning, laundry and dishwashing (I couldn't persuade them to use the dishwasher). I realized how evil Korean culture must be to make virtual slaves out of subordinates and vendors, and them professing adoration of their superiors. It was worse than that. During a visit to our house, the customer (who had refused to join us in my hot tub) explained to my wife that the Korean culture was eight thousand years old, and thus far superior to American culture. They knew better than to let their wives drive cars, as women are too stupid too drive. My wife held back her wrath, she remembered where my paycheck was coming from, but it was hard to take this stuff from a nation of people who had to be rescued from Communism by our American military. This from a nation of people who never invented the chair and thus squatted like monkeys on the street reading the newspaper waiting for the bus.

I eventually finished the training, started to work on the test programs and kept the Koreans happy. Well, not happy, more like mollified. They were upset that someone wasn't working on the test programs while the training was going on and I got the feeling they had expected me to train them by day and write the programs at night. This is the essence of friction between races in my view. Their expectations where wholly different from my obligations. If I had been Korean, I would have known I was expected to work 24 hours a day, but being American, I feel no compunction to kill myself for a lousy paycheck, at least to that degree. Their demands to the contrary rubbed me the wrong way, and my apparent sloth in the performance of what they saw as my *duty* to serve them boiled up as anger towards their lazy American host. When it was time to go back to Korea I only had two of the four test programs written and I knew I could not come home until I had all four working. Yet for some reason I got on that plane. If I had had any sense, I would have quit my job long before that.

My flight over was quite pleasant as my travel agent Bonnie Jell got me a first class upgrade to Korea and back. I gave the return trip upgrade to a friend at Steppenwolf, Fred Spickle, who had been traveling like a madman. That seemed to confuse the ticket agent but it turned out to be OK. I paid $140 for the Cognac I owed to O.K.. On the same flight was the Korean rep, Mr. Rhee, but he had a coach seat. During the flight I persuaded my flight attendant to let the rep ride with me in First Class for a little while, long enough to have a drink with me. When you sit in First Class, you are treated like a king. It wouldn't last long though, I was about to be reduced to slave, even lower than the rep, and it was going to *suck*.

I had planned on being in Korea for two weeks, but the Koreans had other plans. I was to complete the other two test programs and get all four correlated. Little did I know they even had a fifth program planned for me, but they wouldn't tell me about it until later.

I stayed at an extremely opulent hotel way out of downtown Seoul, the Swiss Grande. I even had an executive suite, which meant that I had access to a free happy hour with supposedly all you could drink. It turned out the "host" of this happy hour was a stingy bastard who didn't think you should have more than two glasses of beer in a two hour period. It was like pulling teeth to get a third glass of beer. This guy apparently had never been to an Embassy Suites which served unlimited free beer and wine for three hours every night.

To get to ElectroKook every day I took a taxi. It was expensive, but there was no way I was going to drive with these people on the roads. They broke all the traffic rules, like driving in the bus-only lanes and cutting off busses, forcing their way into traffic when a cop saw them in the bus lane, it was just insanity. I sat in the back of the cab and read my UNIX books, which meant I got really good at UNIX.

In the meantime, I was killing myself at ElectroKook, eating lunch in their **horrible** cafeteria, complete with metal trays like a prison might have. When lunch was over, everyone would file past the scullery area to drop off their dirty trays, grab a small stainless steel cup, fill it with warm water, rinse their mouth, and then spit into a sink. Just watching this ritual while eating made me nauseous. The food was bad enough, kimchi this and kimchi that, with kimchi on the side. I started off liking kimchi, but it was wearing on me.

I was doing amazing work. Most of the programs I wrote worked better, far better than the DactylDyne versions they were running. I even created a semiautomatic calibration procedure for one of the programs that increased accuracy tenfold and demonstrated it to my host. He said, "OK, get back to work on the other program." Ungrateful bastard I thought, this was genius, simply fantastic stuff, but Koreans never complement subordinates on a job well done. This was getting depressing. While I worked all day (about 11 hours) and all night soldering DUT-boards in my hotel room and writing test program code on my "portable" Sun workstation and tried to squeeze one more lousy glass of beer from the Korean happy hour host I got increasingly depressed.

It wasn't all bad, I did end up going out with Mr. Rhee and Mr. Rhee to a SelfHoff. I'm not sure who invented this self serve beer bar but my hat goes off to him. At a SelfHoff you sit at a table with a beer spigot sticking out of the table with a meter that could be configured to read out in liters of beer, or in Won (money). The server gave you as many glasses as you wanted, you fill 'em up yourself and keep an eye on the meter to make sure you don't drink more than you can pay for. Oh my God, did we get drunk! We ordered some dried peas and chopsticks and I challenged the Koreans to a competition, how fast can you eat peas with chopsticks. I won. Maybe they let me win or maybe they were a lot drunker than me, who knows, finally I had some standing with these guys.

I also did some wandering on my own in my spare time. The Koreans had an interesting way of disposing of trash on the street. They would rake it into a heap and then burn it. This had to be city employees doing this. Mostly it was plastic bottles and wrappers so it created these huge plumes of black smoke, not that you could tell, the air was so thick with smog it was hard to see much, even a little additional smog.

Even though the U.S. Army was deeply entrenched in South Korea, I as a white man was quite the novelty. Once I came across a gaggle of Korean school kids. They treated me like some kind of anthropology specimen. One of the kids grabbed a stick and scrawled A B C in the dirt to show that he knew my strange, alien language. Other kids swarmed around me and tugged at the hair on my arms to see if it was real. If they had had cell phones they probably would have all lined up to get a picture with me to post online showing that they had come across a 백인 (baeg-in) and it didn't pick them up and eat them. Koreans are too garlicky for my taste buds anyway.

Another interesting thing I saw was street vendors serving up what I called "road kill squid." The Mr. Rhees had introduced this food item to me in the States. The vendor would setup a charcoal barbecue on the sidewalk and roast dried, flattened squid, which looked like they had driven over to get them flat, hence the name. They tasted like crap. Back in the States I nearly OD'ed on vodka trying to get the taste out of my mouth. No way I was going to touch one of these nasty critters cooked by a guy on the sidewalk.

During an evening outing I was just walking down the street in Itaewon, a "dong" or city district, this pudgy, scruffily dressed Korean gal came up to me and said, "Hey, you wanna fuck?" I declined, thinking to myself *certainly not with you!* Itaewon is where many U.S. Army guys hang out, so being propositioned is not unexpected, but certainly unwelcome, at least in my case.

One night at the hotel bar I enjoyed watching this white couple entertain the Korean patrons. The man was on a keyboard and the beautiful blonde woman sang rock, country, and blues. Then suddenly they started singing the South Korean national anthem in perfect Korean. The reaction by the patrons was instantaneous. They all leapt to their feet and sang along with such emotion I thought I might cry. It was almost as moving as the Marseilles scene in the movie *Casablanca*. That's how you bring down the house in Korea!

While working at ElectroKook in my second week there, my boss got word to me that he needed someone to go to Japan to look at a problem there. The end of my two weeks was coming up and it was going to be Easter weekend. I really wanted to go home to spend Easter with the wife and kids, but one of the test programs was still giving me grief. I made a deal with my boss and the Koreans. They would let me go to Japan for **one day** and I would stay another week to finish the test program that was giving me trouble. That meant giving up Easter with the kids, but I convinced the wife that we could have our own Easter when I got back and somehow convince the youngest kids that the Easter bunny wouldn't forget them a week late.

The Koreans insisted on making my travel arrangements (including my return trip to the States a week later) and taking me to the airport for my flight to Japan. Little did I know they would be meeting me at Kimpo when I came back, just to make sure I *did come back*. They didn't trust me *at all*. I was warned not to try to escape, the customer would be very angry if I did. Boy, these guys certainly were descendants of Genghis Khan, no doubt about it.

While waiting for my flight to Japan I bumped into Jack Davidson, founder of Sanger boats based in Sanger, California. This was quite a coincidence because my mother had lived in Sanger as a kid and graduated from Sanger High School. Since I had recently bought a ski boat from a much cheaper competitor we had a nice chat about ski boats and waterskiing. I couldn't imagine what the founder of Sanger boats might be doing in Korea, but he explained that he was traveling the globe hosting waterski exhibitions. In Korea he had sponsored a waterski exhibition on the Han River, the river that flows from North Korea through Seoul. I could not imagine waterskiing on the Han River. Not only had North Korea threatened to blow up their own dam to flood Seoul downstream of the 38th parallel, I doubted it was clean enough to ski in. I had seen the river plenty of times, and knowing how the Koreans deal with trash made me imagine how they might treat sewage, as in, probably not much at all. No thank you, I'll take the Columbia River over the Han River anytime.

My trip to Japan was a pleasant break from Korea. Japan is a very clean place, cleaner than Korea. I found a female taxi driver who could speak English and was willing to drive me all the way to Tsukuba, a two hour drive. She spoke English very well and after I explained my plans to return to the airport the next day, she asked if I would let her be my taxi driver for the return trip. I agreed and promised to meet her at the customer site the next day. This was quite a commitment because that meant she would have to drive two hours out there to pick me up. I had better not disappoint her, and she had better not disappoint me! If she didn't show up, I might not be able to find a taxi driver to take me all the way back to Tokyo. If that happened I would miss my flight back to Korea and the ElectroKook guys would be super pissed off. The taxi driver and I had to trust each other or it would end badly for both of us. I felt that I could trust this woman, and she, me.

The hotel Ichiban (number one) had the tiniest rooms I had ever seen, the bathroom was slightly larger than an airplane bathroom, but it had to be because it had a shower. The room did have one interesting feature: Japanese TV, complete with X-rated shows after 9PM.

At SIN (Silicon Institute National) the next day I was taken from one section to the next. Every time I had to change into smaller and smaller sandals, so small eventually that they didn't cover my heels. After gowning up in a snug bunny suit and yet another pair of tiny sandals I went onto the test floor to look at the problem. When I admitted to the engineer, an American guy from the States, that I would be leaving that day, he flew off the handle. He was told I would be there until the problem was solved. I couldn't solve his problem, but did correct a few errors that might have prevented him from solving it himself. On leaving SIN at least the Japanese American Steppenwolf rep was grateful, and thanked me. I thought it would be better to stay here than to go back to the hell hole I had just come from, but I had promised the Koreans and the taxi driver that I would be back.

The taxi driver picked me up at SIN as we arranged and took me back to Tokyo to catch my plane. Between her taxi rides at $200 each way and the hotel bill I was almost completely tapped out. I never expected Japan to be so expensive. When I got back to Seoul, Mr Rhee, the Korean rep was waiting for me. He was very relieved that I didn't ditch him and destroy my honor. Give me a break!

Things went downhill from there. I had missed Easter with the kids, and I was depressed. The last test program was proving to be a real problem, I could not get it to pass no matter what I did. I was out of money and sick of the Korean food. One day while having lunch at the ElectroKook cafeteria with the special main course being kimchi soup with kimchi and kimchi side dish with kimchi juice to drink I exploded. I told them no way was I ever eating here again. I was sick of spending my lunch hour watching Koreans spit into a sink, sick of kimchi, sick of the working conditions, spending days and days on the horribly noisy test floor with operators banging nitrogen tanks around and hundreds of machines whirring and clicking and grinding, sick of wearing filthy sandals worn by who knows how many filthy Koreans.

Boy, that did it! They ran out and got me some candy bars, they got me some ESD-safe sneakers so I didn't have to wear sandals and they got me some earplugs to cut down the noise. My host took me to the local bank so I could get some more money. I was so depressed I wouldn't even talk to him, he got the message. He stopped treating me like crap, at least for a few hours.

My departure date was coming up and I was just trying to make it long enough to get on that plane. In my room at the hotel I would look down from my very high window and contemplate jumping. If I did I would crash through the glass lobby roof, very much like the one that Michael Douglas crashed through at the end of his movie, *The Game*. It would be a grand entrance at the Swiss Grande for sure. 부디 God, let me go home!

The Thursday before my departure Mr. Rhee came to me with another data sheet for the fifth chip they wanted me to test. He said that with me leaving on Saturday I was certain to get this one done quickly. The rage in my eyes burning a hole in the back of his skull must have gotten through to him, he said, "I think you can do this one in the U.S.A." He's damn lucky he said that, that might have been his last breath if he hadn't. That Thursday night before my last day at ElectroKook I called the airline to confirm my reservations that the Koreans had made for me the week before. They didn't seem to have a reservation for me. Those *lying bastards!* They had planned to hold me there beyond the third week by simply not making my flight reservations. I tried to get on a flight but that airplane was all booked. I called another airline and told them I had a business class ticket from a competitor and could they get me *the hell out of here* on Saturday? They assured me they could, I had a reservation and I was set to go.

On Friday the customer grudgingly allowed me to leave, with the promise that I would get the new program and the troublesome program both finished and bring them back soon. I would have said anything to get out of there, and that was what I was doing. On Saturday the ElectroKook guys and the rep took me to the airport and thanked me for my work. *It's a little late guys, see ya!*

I had to fly coach the long way, across to Hawaii with a layover, and then one last leg direct to Portland. In Hawaii I basked in the American culture, ate, no, *savored* a Burger King Double Whopper with all my favorite fixings, and just enjoyed my three hour layover hanging out with people who looked and acted like me. It was very refreshing. I was not to return to Korea for over a year, and when I did I was certain I would not get stuck there.

After I got back home the mere mention of Korea would set me off. We got word that ElectroKook, now an independent company wanted that one troublesome test program done. I negotiated with my boss Fran who was very concerned about this project. He wanted to make sure that I didn't get stuck again because I nearly quit after getting back. It was decided that I would spend as much time as was needed to get the program working, no pressure on me, it would be ready when it was ready. I designed a new fixture to solve some of the issues I had run into in Korea, had the boards built, debugged them, wrote calibration and diagnostic programs, integrated the device program with them. I got the program working well and was certain this version would correlate with the competing system's test results. Fran wasn't so sure, but I talked him into letting me go to Korea. He was a good guy who always looked out for his underlings. I should have listened.

I setup for a two week trip, flew over in business class, and was picked up by my old pal, O.K. Dokie, the guy who had lent me money on my first trip over. O.K. was kind of a prick. While conversing he told me he had been promoted from service technician to salesman. His job was **much more important** than my job. I was just a lowly applications engineer, he had skipped over that job directly to sales, he was a truly superior being. O.K. was supposed to take me directly to ElectroKook, but another customer, Songsungblue, needed someone to look at a problem they were having, and since O.K. was not a programmer, he decided to drag me to this customer first. He lied to Mr. Rhee at ElectroKook, telling him that I had gotten off the plane too tired to work and took me straight to my hotel. That didn't work out as well as he hoped. Mr. Rhee called my hotel to speak to me directly and found out I hadn't even checked in yet, and so Mr. Rhee realized he had been lied to. Later O.K. was forced to apologize to Mr. Rhee profusely for lying to him.

In the meantime we arrived at Songsungblue. The customer tried to show me the problem they were having. Well, they sat me down in front of the monitor and expected my mere presence to fix it, but it became obvious that the tester was broken. Since O.K. had been a service technician in his previous life, the customer handed him a screwdriver and told him to fix it. He looked at me and I smiled, "I've never serviced that tester, I'm just a crappy programmer!" O.K. had to eat crow and take up his old craft of fixing testers. It was wonderful. By the end of the day we had figured out the problem, O.K. had gotten a full serving of crow and it was time to go to the Seoul Hilton. O.K. dropped me off, tomorrow he would pick me up and drive me to ElectroKook for our meeting with Mr. Rhee and I would install the new program and hope it all worked.

The next day I met Mr. Rhee, he was cordial, he didn't yell at me for not coming back, that was to come later. I started work on installing the program, got it running and gave him the results. There were some issues, I began to work on them. I worked and I worked and I worked. There was one issue I just could not get past.

As before, I had to take a taxi to get to work every day. The hotel concierge had written the directions to the ElectroKook plant on a card that I was to carry always. It also had directions to the hotel for the taxi drivers to get me back home at the end of the day. Korea doesn't use street addresses, it's more like "go to the Long Dong Wong district and go to the third house on the right." One old taxi driver I got couldn't make out where he was supposed to be taking me. He obviously was lost and was making strange noises (and smells) in the front seat. He stopped the cab, got out and said something to me. When he came back after a few minutes he had vomit on his mouth and **on my travel card**. He apparently went to ask directions and had to throw up, doing so on my card that was the only way I could get back to the hotel. He circled around for a while and finally I recognized the ElectroKook plant grounds and got him to drop me off.

Finally the weekend came, I still had another week, but first I had to put in a half day Saturday, which was normal in Korea. The typical weekend is a day and a half. It is said in Korea that Saturday night is a happy night, the one night of the week Koreans have sex, since they can sleep in on Sunday. Come on boys, if it takes that much out of you, you're doing it wrong.

One of the ElectroKook guys who could barely speak English had volunteered to entertain me on Sunday, so the next day he swung by the hotel and drove me up to the thirty-eighth parallel, the border with North Korea. There was a visitor center there called Imjingak Resort, complete with an observation area high on a hilltop. Inside the visitor center is a scale model of Kijong-dong, a real life "Potemkin Village" visible on the North Korean side of the border. This was supposed to be a real North Korean city, but the visitor center made it clear that it was a total hoax. The NK government employed actors to make it look like a real city, so it was almost like *The Truman Show* with artificial activity buzzing around this fake city, built here only because they knew the South Koreans were looking at them from this hilltop. At the visitor center there was a store where you could buy North Korean products, a beer brewed in North Korea, cigarettes manufactured in North Korea and a North Korean whiskey. I bought a can of beer as a souvenir.

As we walked out to the parking lot I could hear voices calling out from loudspeakers visible on the NK side. I asked my host what it said. It was the North Koreans calling to the South Koreans to leave the evil capitalist society and join the workers paradise on the NK side. I laughed at that, but then he pointed out the speakers on the South Korea side pointed north. "We are doing the same thing!" he exclaimed. Too funny!

The next week was tense, again I had a deadline, my flight was scheduled to leave on Saturday, and I *still* couldn't get this damn thing to correlate. Fran was right, I was going to get stuck there again because I was too proud to stay in the U.S. longer to make *damn sure* this thing was going to work. Too much optimism is a bad thing.

On Wednesday I confronted Mr. Rhee and told him I might have to return to the States to finish, then come back. He said, "When will you come back, in a year?" That hurt, but I couldn't blame him. He talked me into doing something a little unethical, putting in a fudge factor to get the program to pass. Apparently they do it all the time, my integrity prevented me from even thinking such a thing, but he had no problem with it.

We had another problem, it was springtime in Korea, which meant some kind of social unrest. Years ago my mentor, the inestimable Sy Johnson had warned me about traveling to Korea during *Protest Season*. He had walked through streets where tear gas wafted between the buildings and had to stay in his hotel for days on end to avoid the violence and unrest. Now it was my turn. There was some sort of labor dispute with the operators at ElectroKook. One day at least a hundred of them sat in the middle of the test floor blocking operations. They sat in hallways, they carried signs outside the building, and they wrote slogans on the walls with markers.

On Thursday morning the operators were holding a rally outside the plant grounds, good sign I thought, they aren't in the building. Wrong assumption, they had been locked out by management, which meant they were preparing to storm the building. Mr. Rhee told me (for the hundredth time I am guessing) to get the program working immediately, I would have to leave soon before the violence started. I got the program working well, then I was recruited to help barricade the test floor against the coming onslaught of angry operators. We moved one of the testers up against a door and piled boxes on top to keep them from climbing over it. We blocked other doors with nitrogen tanks, boxes, whatever we could move. Mr. Rhee told me it was time to go, thanks so much, have a nice flight, see ya! You don't have to tell me twice Mr. Rhee, I was outta there before you could say Kamsahamnida, if you could say it.

Years later I figured out what had given me so much trouble with that device. It was a little understood issue called Sin(X)/X that reduces the amplitude of a signal when you have a limited sample rate. If I had understood this issue I would not have had as much trouble with this one test program. So this time, it was my fault.

I was quite leery of going to Korea after that, for any reason whatsoever. Many flights I took going to Asia went through Seoul and I imagined one of the Mr. Rhee's lurking in the Kimpo airport waiting to catch me on my way to Taiwan or China. Some time later I ended up with a project that would end in me delivering a test program to Gumi, Korea.

The chip was designed by a company in San Jose called Cro-Magnon (which later became part of TIA) but S&M in Korea was going to produce it and they were a new customer at the time. I was asked to fly to Seoul to meet the S&M folks, discuss the project and give a training class. I was nervous.

I gave the training class and it went very well, the Koreans in the class were quite friendly and competent. They were even helpful when I suffered a rather serious nose bleed on the test floor due to the very low humidity in the airplane on the flight. My nose was gushing blood all over the test floor, the Koreans mopping it up with paper towels, it was embarrassing, but I survived and they felt sympathetic to my plight.

Then I had a meeting with a Mr. Abe about the project, called PinkyPact!. The exclamation point was part of the name, kind of like the TV game show Jeopardy!. It was a video chip that used a new bus protocol called RAMBUS, way too fast for the tester that S&M had bought, but someone convinced S&M that it would work (probably So Ree Jack, that sneaky little devil).

Mr. Abe asked how we planned to test the RAMBUS, I explained that we had decided in meetings with the Cro-Magnon people that it didn't need to be tested. Mr. Abe totally flew off the handle, he came completely unglued! He started screaming that this needed to be tested, he started drawing diagrams with nonsensical topologies showing how he would test it if **he** were the engineer. He pounded his fist on his desk and told me, "You will not leave Korea until I am satisfied with the test strategy!" Well, given what I had been through with ElectroKook, that went over like a lead balloon. I got myself out of there quickly but Mr. Abe *ordered me* not to leave Korea.

When I got to the hotel I put in an angry call to the salesman for S&M. He was a fairly calm guy and listened intently as I ranted that I would not stay in Korea just to make Mr. Abe happy. He told me very calmly that I should just "ignore Mr. Abe's request." I thought to myself *you mean I can do that?* He told me he would take care of it, don't worry, you are leaving on schedule. Back in the States when I heard I was going to Korea I had started joking with people that I should pack an inflatable raft in my bags so I could paddle to China if I got nabbed again by crazy Koreans. Now here is a Korean who told me it's OK to ignore the customer and go home as scheduled. Damn, I sure wish someone had told me I could do that last time! So it was OK, our salesman straightened things out with Mr. Abe and I went home to work on the project.

Several months later I had the program working and ready to be installed, which meant another trip to Korea. However this time my boss gave me strict orders, I was *not* to deviate from the plan, I was **not** to say yes to any requests for me to stay on. My Korean rep was given the same instructions. This came about in part due to my previous trip to Taiwan where I had threatened to quit if they didn't let me go home. The Koreans had also mistreated another of our applications engineers to the point that he threatened to quit. Management had learned a lesson. Good!

I flew to Seoul and visited the customer, S&M. Again it was Mr. Abe. He was filled in on the test program, requirements, features, etcetera. Then I was told we would not be installing the program at Seoul, it was to be installed at the plant in Gumi, a three hour drive down the center of Korea. I was instructed to give the program tape to some of the test engineers and they would transfer it electronically to Gumi, the program would be there by the time I arrived. I hoped they didn't lose that tape. Later I realized I should have been more careful with the tape.

As my rep drove me down there I noticed something curious about this highway. It was two lanes each way with a paved median and a removable barrier between directions. I asked why they did it that way. The answer was that since North Korea and South Korea are still technically at war, they have to be ready for the war to resume at any time. If needed, the barrier can be removed and the highway can be used as a runway for military aircraft for its entire length. It's hard to imagine being in a state of war all the time, kind of messes with your head.

Now, while Gumi might make you think of Gummi Bears, it is quite the opposite of such pleasant things. It is a purely industrial town filled with belching smokestacks, grinding poverty and filthy everything. I realized Seoul was the garden spot of Korea. Kind of like going to a dump, which you thought was bad, then being buried in garbage and realizing there are worse things than standing **on** garbage.

Luckily I wasn't going to have to stay here, especially in the gloomy Gumi Prince Hotel. I had heard plenty of horror stories from my coworkers who had been sentenced to spend time here. All I had to do was have lunch here before we went to the S&M plant. Just "dining" here was enough to tell me I never wanted to set foot in here again.

At the S&M plant Mr. Abe was waiting. It seems the intranet connection between Gumi and Seoul had gone down and might not be up again till the next day. The program that I had brought to Korea on tape, which the Koreans in Seoul had taken from me, could not be transferred today. Mr. Abe had decided to tell the engineers in Seoul to bring the tape down so I could install the program. This all came down around 2PM. The guys from Seoul would not be here till 5PM, my flight back home left the next morning, I had to get back to Seoul that evening so I could catch my flight the next day.

Mr. Abe didn't see it that way. He seemed to think I could pull an all-nighter, get the program installed and running, then get back to Seoul and catch my plane. I was only going to sleep on the plane anyway, what would I lose. *My fucking mind, that's what* I thought to myself. I told him no, I was staying on schedule, and that was that. He stood there, head lowered, slowly shaking his head and breathing through his teeth. In Korea this is a sign of disapproval, I was bordering on shameful disobedience. I was getting really good at reading these Koreans.

As Mr. Abe continues breathing through his teeth for the next twenty minutes let me relate to you what I was told about Korean workplace etiquette and seniority. Apparently you are expected to rise through the ranks to the top, no matter what your skills or temperament. It was said that if you celebrated your fortieth birthday and were still not a manager, the next day at work, your desk would be gone and in its place would be a broom. You were expected to take the broom and sweep the floors until you retired. No further explanation was needed.

Finally, Mr. Abe quit breathing through is teeth and said, "OK." The engineers from Seoul had arrived with the tape, they would install it, check it out, solve any problems and get it into production. I thanked them profusely. *Kamsahamnida! Kamsahamnida!* As I thought to myself *I am outta here!*

After that trip I started looking for another job. I wasn't going back there, even if I had escaped without having to pull an all-nighter. Later in my role as Marketing Applications Engineer for TestEz, I visited Korea with Olie Lee, a Korean American who also worked for TestEz with whom I was fairly friendly, along with our sales guy Lam Thong, my Chinese American friend from TestEz. I had already warned Olie Lee that I was no fan of Korea and I was prepared to ditch the two of them if I had to escape. Since I had already pulled such a stunt on Lam Thong in Taiwan, he knew I wasn't kidding, I was taken seriously. Olie promised there would be no trouble.

We picked up the local rep, another Mr. Lee and went to Songsungblue to speak to them (another pair of Mr. Lees) about mixed signal test which they were mildly interested in. We went out to lunch, more kimchi, OK, I can handle a little. Then we were told that the next round of talks would be in Korean and had nothing to do with me and Lam, so they would take us to a nearby hotel and Day Spa where they had traditional Korean hot spring baths. Well, that sounded good to me, I had a hot tub at home that I loved, but Lam was a little less enthusiastic.

When we got there our rep told us to leave all our stuff in the trunk of his car, except for the fee for the baths. They did have lockers, but we were told you can't trust them to stay locked, everyone in the country has a key! In other words the Korean is telling us that Koreans are untrustworthy. OK, that's fine I guess, but again, Lam didn't like it. He couldn't live without his cell phone and laptop, Type A personality you know.

So we pay our fee and go to the dressing room. We have to do this naked, and honestly I hadn't thought about it before now. Well, you have to respect other cultures I guess (liberal nonsense seeping into my brain, make it stop). So now I have to get naked in front of my coworker Lam, who is sort of my superior. Of course being Asian he wasn't superiorly endowed, so that helped. We put on our only apparel, flip flops, and walked to the baths.

This place looked great! It had a whole wall of open showers that must have spewed ten gallons a minute each. There were four different baths, one mineral bath with a greenish tint, very hot. Three more at different temperatures and concoctions, and a steam room! I was game, I showered thoroughly first (hoping everyone else did likewise) then jumped in and enjoyed the hot water. Lam did too. We tried the green pool, too hot. I went into the steam room for a few minutes and when I came out I realized that Lam was gone. No matter, we were told we had a couple of hours to waste so I bounced between pools and showers trying not to notice that I was the most well endowed guy in the place. No wonder these Koreans only have sex on Saturday night. It probably takes all week just to find it again. I was treated like a gifted porn star in Korea. Once while using the restroom in Kimpo, a Korean cleaning lady came by to have a surreptitious look at my "gift" while trying to pretend to use a feather duster to clean the urinal I was using. Honestly, it's a lot like dealing with children.

Finally I tired of the baths, got dressed and went looking for Lam. He was upstairs in the hotel business center using one of their PCs to check his email. Type A for sure! The poor guy was lost without his laptop and cell phone, he was going crazy, and boy was he pissed off. I thought, well *it's about time one of you guys finds Korea insufferable, especially an Asian.* He said that he wanted to go to the bar to get something to drink after being dehydrated from the heat of the baths but he didn't have any money, no credit card and of course, because we weren't staying here, he couldn't charge it to his room!

He was like a fish out of water. I liked Lam, but I had to admit, I was pleased. Lam had never been an applications engineer, had never had to endure what these Koreans could dish out. At least he was suffering a little bit, even if it was just a matter of inconvenience, he *had* to suffer some, it was only fair.

Eventually our hosts came back to pick us up and we had a couple of beers at the hotel bar. Lam got his wallet, phone and laptop back, he was happy. We left Seoul and drove out of the new airport at Incheon, about 40 miles west of Seoul. This is the direction I would have had to go if I had packed a life raft with me and had to escape to China. Sort of out of the pot and into the fire so to speak. It was a maze of estuaries, easy enough to negotiate in a rubber raft. Always thinking about an escape plan, look at what traveling has done to me!

We had flown into this airport but had little time to investigate it until now. It was bigger than the old Seoul airport, Kimpo. The humorous thing was that it was an **exact replica** of Kimpo, I could even see the place where I had said goodbye to the Mr. Rhees from ElectroKook years earlier, even though I knew that place was forty miles east of here, it looked exactly the same. The immigration officer looked at my passport, I climbed aboard the plane and said goodbye to Korea. Kamsahamnida God for letting me leave this place again.

I never went back to Korea, I have no desire to go back to Korea. However on one trip to San Jose while having lunch in a sushi restaurant I noticed a familiar sounding banter between the chef and the waitress, presumably his wife. The sushi was good, so on my way out the door I looked at her and said, "Kamsahamnida!" She beamed with a big smile, sighed and started speaking in Korean. I waved my hand and shook my head communicating very clearly *that's the only word I know lady, thanks just the same.*

I'm getting closer to my home
I'm getting closer to my home
I'm getting closer to my home
I'm getting closer to my home
I'm getting closer to my home
I'm getting closer to my home
I'm getting closer to my home
I'm getting closer to my home
I'm getting closer to my home
I'm getting closer to my home
I'm getting closer to my home
I'm getting closer to my home
I'm getting closer to my home
I'm getting closer to my home
I'm getting closer to my home
I'm getting closer to my home
I'm getting closer to my home
I'm getting closer to my home
I'm getting closer to my home
I'm getting closer to my home
I'm getting closer to my home
I'm getting closer to my home
I'm getting closer to my home
I'm getting closer to my home
I'm getting closer to my home
I'm getting closer to my home
I'm getting closer to my home

I'm Your Captain by Grand Funk Railroad

China

"Don't worry, built by the French"
Assurance by my host that the tram to the top of the Great Wall is safe.

My first trip to China was not to Communist China, but to Hong Kong which was taken from the Chinese in 1842 with the Treaty of Nanking following the Opium Wars to open up China to trade with Britain. In 1860 Britain coerced Beijing into ceding Kowloon on the mainland, and then in 1898 they succeeded in gaining the New Territories and outlying islands including Lantu Island.

My job was not to invade Hong Kong, but to teach a class on the Axmi AX100 and SOS3000 that I had recently learned about to several test engineers at the RotoMolded facility in Kowloon. Except for a brief trip to Canada to help Southern Morse in Ottowa, and my onetime journey to Australia with the U.S. Navy, I had never been out of the U.S.

I ran off the manuals I would need and then shipped them to RotoMolded Hong Kong. I flew over on Friday afternoon and landed fifteen hours later on Saturday night at Kai Tak airport in Hong Kong. This was a really scary place to land. Hong Kong is very mountainous and planes coming into Kai Tak had to almost dive out of the sky, do a slalom course through the skyscrapers in Kowloon and then set down and jam on the brakes to make sure they didn't shoot off the end of the runway and crash into Hong Kong harbor. Hong Kong didn't have a sewage treatment plant, everything went straight into the harbor, so landing in the water, which sometimes happened, meant that even if you survived the crash, you would have to be inoculated against about a dozen nasty diseases.

However, our landing went well, I even got to watch a few people taking showers in their bathrooms through the window of the plane as we approached. After collecting my bags I found some buses that took visitors to the various hotels and bought a ticket. Somehow I got in the wrong line and ended up on the wrong bus. I got an informal tour of the New Territories, but when we hit the last stop I asked the driver, "Park Hotel?" "Wrong bus" he exclaimed. We parked for a while so the driver could smoke a cigarette and then he drove me back to Kai Tak airport so I could get on the **right** bus to take me to the Park Hotel in Kowloon.

This was a swanky place! It was right in downtown Kowloon so there were fancy shops everywhere with lots to see and do. I got some sleep and then went out on Sunday to figure out where I had to go to teach the class at RotoMolded. I talked to the hotel concierge and he gave me a map of the area and highlighted the place I was supposed to be. I figured out how to use the subway, the MTR, or Mass Transit Railway. It was very clean, cheap and easy to use. I made sure I learned the name of the stop I was at, Tsim Sha Tsui so that I could find my way back to the hotel. I jumped on the train and found the stop I needed to get off at. I walked around and found the RotoMolded building where I was expected tomorrow. This was going to be a piece of cake! I took the MTR back to Tsim Sha Tsui (listen for it, listen for it) and successfully completed a full round trip to and from the RotoMolded building.

Now that I was in good shape there, I looked around to form a mental map of my surroundings. This place was great! Really cool shops all over the place, restaurants, bars, jewelry stores, everything you could want and more. They even had a McDonald's just down the street from the hotel near the MTR station. Since I was on foot, there was no need to worry about traffic, and unlike Taiwan (which I had not been to yet) there were almost no scooters. Just fairly sedate car, taxi and bus traffic. It was really very livable and I was certain I was going to enjoy my time here.

I had been told that Hong Kong was a great place for shopping, so I planned ahead and brought a fair bit of cash. Things were so cheap, I could really splurge and still get away without spending much money. I bought freshwater pearl necklaces for sisters-in-law, I bought silk kimonos for my wife, myself, my kids and my nieces and nephews. I bought gaudy rings, toys, silk ties (which only cost $1 each), all kinds of stuff. I was in shopper's heaven, and even though I wasn't really a shopper, it was hard to resist the plethora of trinkets, clothes, watches and jewelry that people were hawking all up and down every street.

Of course I was there to work, not shop. On Monday morning I took my briefcase full of slides, paper and pens, books and calculators and made my way on the MTR to RotoMolded's building. They only occupied floors 7-14 of this 32 story building, so I got on the elevator with a whole bunch of Chinese people. The doors stayed open as people continued to board the elevator. Finally a buzzer went off. One person got off, the buzzer stopped, and the doors closed. We were at full capacity, and I prayed to God that this elevator could handle running at full capacity day after day after day. It did, but it was unnerving.

On the seventh floor was a receptionist, so I asked to see Mr. Liu, and he promptly appeared. He greeted me warmly and we made our way to the classroom. I asked about the boxes of books, but he had not yet seen them, so went looking for them. I got my stuff together and began meeting the students as they swarmed into the room. Very friendly folks, all of them. Mr. Liu came back without the books. He would go look for them again in a couple of hours after the mail delivery truck arrived.

Until then I had to entertain these folks. I tried talking about myself for a while, told a few jokes, talked about the tester I had only recently been introduced to myself, and the company where I had only recently started working. I was *dying* here, but then Mr. Liu came back from the mailroom with boxes and boxes of books. Thank God! Now we can get to work.

From then on the class went well. I talked with some very smart people (this was RotoMolded after all, they only hired smart people) and learned a lot about what they did there. One thing they did was probe wafers using their AX100 tester. Probing is quite delicate stuff, probes are placed by the micron, not the inch, so precision and stability are crucial.

Strangely I noticed this pounding, like one beat per second shaking the whole building. It was especially noticeable in the stairwell, but you couldn't escape it. I asked about it and was told that there was a tool making shop in the offices above RotoMolded's eight floors. They had some kind of metal forming press that pounded steel into some shape or another. I thought it was odd that they could successfully probe semiconductor wafers with all that pounding, but they did, so who am I to worry about it?

The AX100 had an incredibly slow computer running UNIX. So while the lecture time went well, the labs that we did were painfully slow. They only had one AX100 that we could use, the rest were busy in production. When a student wanted to compile a program, you could count on waiting fifteen minutes before the compile was done. Then loading the program would take another ten to fifteen minutes. So one try at the program would take you a half hour, and then if you made a mistake in your Pascal, you would have to edit the code, and try again. It took a really long time to get through the labs. We resorted to retiring to the cafeteria and drinking coffee while the computer compiled the program (why does this sound familiar) and then go back to check for errors, fix any that popped up, or load the program if the compile was successful, then return to the cafeteria for more coffee to let the program load.

We had all our lunches in the cafeteria on site, and the food was quite good. I was partial to Chinese food anyway and this place did not disappoint. One day I was told that the cafeteria was serving a very special dish for lunch. I couldn't imagine what it was, so I asked. Pigeon!

Now realize, this is Hong Kong, and it's not easy to find a knife and fork, so I had worked really hard at learning to use chopsticks to eat all my meals, except breakfast at the hotel. Hard to eat eggs over easy with chopsticks. I did well eating the pigeon with my chopsticks. My hosts would occasionally ask me if I wanted a fork, but I was determined to use only chopsticks.

So every day I would take the MTR to the RotoMolded plant, teach, sit in the cafeteria for hours during lab time, and ride the MTR back home to Tsim Sha Tsui and relax in the hotel for a bit before going out on the town. It was really hard not to just roam around looking at all the stuff people were selling! After a while, I got used to who was selling what, and a tiny bit of the fun vaporized, especially the second week.

On Friday I was given some ideas of how to spend the weekend. One thing that I **had** to do was to go over to Hong Kong Island and take the cogwheel tram to the top of Victoria Peak, the tallest mountain in the area with a very well maintained park and walking paths. Instead of taking the MTR to Hong Kong I took a ferry boat from Kowloon across the harbor. The lower deck was only 10 cents Hong Kong, but for a little more you could ride on the upper deck and avoid getting that nasty harbor water splashed on you.

The ride up the cogwheel railway was great. Once on Victoria Peak, I was breathless from the enormity of the view in front of me, or maybe it was the thick smog that blanketed the whole area. It was beautiful though, the city was rich, vibrant, pulsing with life. Human life only, the only birds I saw were the ones I was stuffing into my mouth.

Speaking of which, there were chickens everywhere. I noticed many vendors with cages full of chickens on the street, and on top of the cages was a cookstove powered by butane. The chickens were being cooked just inches above the heads of their friends who were also about to make the journey to Chicken Heaven by way of a Chinaman's stomach.

The food stores had trays full of tofu out on the sidewalk, and with people walking by and spitting every chance they got, it was hard not to be grossed out thinking about having that tofu in my Hot and Sour soup. I only got sick once, and it was from Salmonella poisoning at a regular, sit down restaurant just around the corner from the Park Hotel. It hit me in the middle of my second Wednesday night there. By Thursday morning I was in really bad shape. Luckily, I had Mr. Liu's phone number so I called and told him I would not be in this Thursday. He asked if I needed a doctor, but I declined. It was just stomach trouble, I would be fine by the end of the day, or at least I hoped I would.

I recovered, but of course I lost one day out of 10 days of training. We didn't get to do our final lab project, but the class was happy they had gotten what they did, and they were very appreciative. They took me out to a Dim Sum place for a celebratory class lunch on Friday. This was a real treat! There were all these ladies pushing carts full of different kinds of dumplings up and down between the tables. They would try to talk you into this one, or that one, or this other one, it was fantastic. It all tasted so good, I pigged out, which I needed to anyway because I hadn't had anything to eat the previous day what with my stomach doing belly flops after the salmonella chicken fiasco.

I thanked my hosts for bringing me over to Hong Kong. I and they had both learned a lot. Now I had to get myself and my suitcase full of silk, gold and pearl treasures back to the U.S.A. The takeoff from Kai Tak was much less frightening than the landing and after fourteen hours, we landed in LAX and I got through customs without a hitch. A short flight to San Jose and I was home with stories to tell and gifts to give out. I also had that trip to Southern Morse to deal with, which, as you know now, did not go nearly as well as my trip to Hong Kong.

I made many other trips to Hong Kong. Since So Ree Jack lived in Hong Kong, he would sometimes bring me there to just to have someone to hang out with. One time we took the ferry to Lantu Island, home of the Po Lin Buddhist monastery and one of the largest statues of Buddha in the world. The ferry took us from Kowloon to Lantu Island, then a bus took us up to the mountaintop monastery and from then on we were welcome to walk around the grounds and climb the stairs to the giant Tian Tan Buddha. It was big, quite a sight to be sure.

Then So Ree decided it was time for lunch, but before I ate I wanted to wash my hands. I had touched a million filthy things since I left the hotel. The ferry was filthy, even on the upper deck, the bus was filthy, the porta-potties were filthy, and yet there was no running water anywhere to wash your hands! There was no solution, so we just went to the monastery diner and sat down at a table with a gaggle of strangers. The waitstaff brought out rice and various dishes and everyone took it family style. What really grossed me out was that everyone would use the chopsticks they had just put in their mouths to dig food from the common rice bowl and other plates of food, so that everything was contaminated in a giant version of communal double dipping. Again, I decided the best course of action was to drink as much beer as possible to kill whatever parasites, bacteria and viruses might end up in my stomach. "Tsingtao!" I cried, and even here, in this mountaintop monastery, I could get a Tsingtao beer.

Much later, Kai Tak airport was replaced with a new airport on Chek Lap Kok Island which is very, very close to Lantu Island. A short bridge connects the airport to Lantu Island. A major highway with an adjoining MTR line now runs along the shore of Lantu Island where that old bus used to run carrying tourists to see the Buddha, and then a very long causeway connects Lantu Island to Tsing Yi Island, and finally Kowloon and the New Territories. Lantu Island is no longer isolated by the harbor, you don't need to take a ferry to see the giant Buddha. Just drive down the causeway or jump on the MTR and you are there! I'm sorry, even with the dirty old buses and the dirty old ferries, I prefer to remember Lantu Island the way it was, when it was an ordeal to get there and not just a short ride on the MTR, a bus or a taxi. Oh, the price of progress.

I made only one trip to China proper. My trips to Hong Kong and Taiwan prepared me some, but I was much less prepared than I thought. My assignment was to go to Shanghai and Beijing (Peking) to install test programs that I had written for various devices that the Aerospace, Ballistics and Ordinance Ministry (ABOM) had asked for. ABOM was the Chinese version of NASA in the U.S., but I quickly found it to be far less impressive than NASA.

I flew in to Hong Kong, then took a short flight to Beijing, there being no direct flights to China from the U.S.. I was accompanied by a really great guy, Fred Cabana who is a Filipino American and grew up in Hawaii. We flew together, so for once I was not going to be stuck in a foreign country alone. This time I got to hang out with a good friend, which was such a blessing!

I was used to bureaucracy when traveling overseas, but right away I knew China was going to take it to a whole new level. I had to show my passport everywhere, from the money exchange to the hotel, to taxi drivers, everyone wanted to see my passport. The reason for this was so that the Communist government could track me throughout the country.

When I changed money, I found that I had exchanged my U.S. Dollars for a pile of special currency called *Foreign exchange certificates* or FEC, that was only usable by foreigners, whereas the general population used Renminbi. According to the government, the two were mutually exclusive. It was illegal for me to pay for something with dollars, and I was not allowed to hold Renminbi. This was a structure that prevented smuggling and black markets. For this reason there were only a few stores I could visit. There were entire department stores *Friendship Stores* that catered only to foreigners, locals were not allowed in. To screen out locals you had to show your passport to get inside. It seemed like a very inefficient system and likely to cause jealousy and hatred of foreigners, but I tried to treat it all as an observer, not a troublemaker, especially in a country that routinely jails troublemakers for years and is said to harvest organs from prisoners. I was going to be very careful here.

However, I did do one thing that might have gotten me in trouble. I brought with me a small hardcover edition of George Orwell's Animal Farm. I toyed with the idea of getting someone in Immigration to give me an entry stamp in my book, but I changed my mind at the last minute which might have saved my freedom. However, I did make a point of carrying it with me everywhere in my inside coat pocket. Look at the cover, upper right picture. It's right there in my inside breast pocket of the parka I am wearing on the Great Wall of China.

The day after arriving in Beijing, Fred and I were picked up at our hotel and taken by taxi to the ABOM main campus. The site was huge, and was surrounded by blocks of apartment buildings where the workers at the facility lived. You were not allowed to live anywhere else if you worked at ABOM. That way they didn't have to have bus service and worry about people not showing up for work. You had no excuse, you lived within walking distance of work, you damn well had better show up!

In the lobby of ABOM we got our visitors badges made and approved by some apparatchik, again having to hand over our passports to be scrutinized and copied. While we waited we noticed glass display cases of model rockets showing the various missiles they were building or had built in the past. The models were poorly constructed, looking more like Estes model rocket kits built by eight year old boys. The facilities were very shabby too, and this was the main lobby! This did not bode well for our stay and proved to be a telling indicator of the state of China's ABOM.

We were marched over to another building while we noted large missile fuselages laying about on the ground between the buildings. Some had been damaged by explosions or fires. We walked past huge heaps of trash including food garbage that, in winter probably didn't smell at all, but imagine summertime! Whew! As I mentioned before, in Taiwan they pile up the trash in bags. Here, no bags.

When we got to the building we would be working in, both Fred and I just stood there slack-jawed. It was like visiting Detroit. Everything was shabby and in a horrible state of disrepair. In one hallway you could see large areas of unpainted concrete and, like a slice of a tree, you could count the layers of paint that had been applied over the years. Probably "make-work" for some poor guy who needed something to do. One day while working in a lab I heard this big crash, like someone breaking dishes in the hallway. I went out to see what the commotion was all about. On the floor lay the shards of a large slab of paint that had fallen off the wall and crashed to the floor leaving a patch of unpainted concrete on the wall. Another indicator was the "toilet," which we call the bathroom. They did have one sit-down toilet in a stall with a single 40 W bare light bulb dangling from the ceiling. There was no toilet paper, but there was a pile of newsprint that you could read until you were done with your business, then wipe with it. Don't flush it! Oh no! The system can't handle that, just put the dirty newsprint in the waste basket. So of course there was this horrific stench from all the wipings of who knows how many Chinese butts left to linger in the stall. The women's toilet was the same, but there was also this trickle of blood streaming out of the doorway towards a floor drain. We all know the source of this blood, but why would it be running down the floor? Who knows? I didn't bother investigating.

I brought several test programs for some very interesting devices that would end up in Chinese missiles. One of the most interesting devices was a LogAnaChip Voltage to Frequency Convertor. This device puts out a free running clock proportional in frequency to the input voltage. LogAnaChip claimed it was linear to 16 bits, meaning that the output frequency would linearly track the input voltage with one part in 65,536 (64K) steps. When I wrote the test program I found that I could not prove this even though our tester was perfectly capable (theoretically) of measuring this. No matter what I did I could not get it to give me this performance. I even asked LogAnaChip for help but their advice was, "Don't try." Well, that was the best I could do, so I had to go to China with that result.

The other problem I had was that if I had done the test in the traditional way, ramping through all 65,536 steps it would take hours to test one chip. I was used to test times in seconds, not hours, so I came up with a brilliant solution. I ramped the voltage up in an exponential curve so that I would cover the range in fewer test steps and much less time. It was a brilliant technique and I was really proud of having come up with it. I was really eager to teach this technique to the Chinese engineers at ABOM. I found a few other shortcuts for other devices that made the test program and test hardware more reasonable. I was really looking forward to showing off my brilliance.

So I installed the test programs while 30 to 60 Chinese engineers (people faded in and out of the sessions) looked on. I tried to get some of them to help me but it was no use. It seemed they were afraid of even touching the keyboard and mouse. I found out later that was probably a good thing. They just were not competent at UNIX which was the OS that the testers ran on. Once I got the programs installed, I demonstrated them to the students, they looked on in wonder and awe.

Later we were each given a classroom and Fred and I spent several days teaching the engineers how the programs worked, doing code walkthroughs and showing off the schematics, etcetera. The engineers, all degreed, understood none of it. They fought me on the simplest points. They really didn't understand my exponential curve for the V-to-F convertor, they wanted it linear. When I explained that the test program would run for hours they backed off a little but they still didn't trust it because they didn't understand how to calculate linearity based on an exponential curve. I gave in and modified the code to make it default to linear to placate them but it took all the fun out of it. Besides, with a 2 hour test time, it makes more work for someone who needs a job, right? "Hey you! Stare into space for two hours and if the light turns green, put the chip there, and if it turns red, put it there. Got it?"

On another test program for an analog switch they argued with me about my approach to an On-state leakage test. The data sheet required that the input be connected to the output with a relay to test leakage. However, I reasoned that since the chip was essentially an electronic relay that was supposed to be ON anyway, I could just tell the switch to be ON and it was the same thing as having an external relay, but without the extra components and the parasitic leakage those components would have added. I could not get them to understand that my approach was identical to the approach used in the data sheet, they would not listen. I was beginning to be really glad that no one I knew would be going up in a Chinese rocket given these people's very limited understanding of electronics.

Fred and I worked hard every day at our jobs and he was equally frustrated with his guys and gals, but at least he only had to try to teach them digital which is a bit simpler than what I was teaching them. At lunchtime, instead of going out to eat, the Chinese would bring in some "box lunch" in a disposable flip-top Styrofoam box. Most often it was white rice, some kind of vegetable like Bok Choy and some meat bits marinated in some kind of sauce. Most of the time it was edible, but one day while eating, Fred fumed in anger after he found a spiral metal shaving in his food, like what you might get when drilling metal. Fred was really mad! He came close to eating this piece of metal and although he was really hungry refused to eat any more of the lunch. From then on Fred never ate the lunches they brought us.

One day I was working on making a modification to a circuit board and asked for a soldering iron, a little solder and some wire. I was given a a soldering iron reminiscent of the one I used to solder my 1968 Cadillac radiator. It must have been a 1000 Watt iron with a half inch diameter tip, way more heat than I could use. That much heat could damage my very expensive circuit board but I was assured that this was all they had. For the wire, they fished some wire out of the garbage and handed it to me. This wire used the old style insulation that melted when the wire gets hot, so it was impossible to solder the wire and end up with anything other than a really ratty looking connection. It had to do, this was all they had. After that I always carried a small butane powered soldering iron with me. You never know what the customer might have, or not have when you get where you are going.

So by day we fought with the engineers, and by night we roamed the city of Beijing with our hosts who worked for the local distributor. We waded through ankle deep trash in the heart of the city to a place that served Peking Duck. It was good, but true to what you see at the end of the classic movie *A Christmas Story*, they cook the duck with the head on it. Then they split it down the middle opening up the skull. Our hosts insisted that I eat the duck brain, which I was told was a delicacy, but I noticed that I was the only one "honored" enough to eat the brain. No one else wanted any. Strange.

Sometimes Fred and I would wander without our hosts and see the sights. I was plagued with people constantly offering me "CD ROM! CD ROM!" or "DVD!" Pirated music, movies or software for the white guy walking down the street. I noticed that no one offered anything like this to Fred. Being a Filipino they probably figured he had no money and they might have thought that Fred was my servant. Not so, Fred and I were peers, and Fred was a really good engineer and fun to have around. Fred is very much a clean freak, even more than me, and it was entertaining to see him "overreact" to the insane stuff we saw. For example, during the week we would walk down this one street where there was this huge grease spot on the pavement, but we had no idea why it seemed to grow and change day to day. Come Saturday we noticed that by day there was a Mongolian BBQ cart in that spot and the proprietor would just dump his used cooking grease right on the street by his cart. Fred was disgusted! We talked to someone about this and were told that was one reason to keep your eyes open when wandering around China. Very often some enterprising person would steal a cast iron manhole cover and turn it into a BBQ grill. Of course that meant that there would be a hole in the street where this manhole cover had been and unsuspecting tourists wandering the streets had been known to fall straight into the hole falling into the sewer below the street.

Another thing we noticed was the ubiquitous Chinese Red Army soldiers lining the streets, complete with very old looking single shot rifles. I asked my host about this and worried aloud about getting shot. He told me, "Don't worry, no bullets!" More busy work I guess. Another thing that bothered Fred was the constant headaches and shortness of breath that plagued him since our arrival. Eventually we figured it out. People were burning coal to stay warm and so the air was filled with carbon monoxide. This is a gas that can kill you, and it was very much affecting our ability to breath and think so it was getting near toxic levels, but there was little we could do about it.

Finally we were going to have some fun. Our hosts took us to Tiananmen Square, site of the Freedom Protests of 1989. The Square is bordered on all sides by interesting landmarks. The Forbidden City is on one side, the Chinese Parliament on another, and Mao's Tomb was nearby. I was carrying my copy of Animal Farm so I had to pay homage to the bastard who killed 60 million of his own people through starvation, torture and forced labor. I was amused that I could see the "Golden Arches" of a nearby McDonald's down the road. That must have Mao spinning in his grave.

We got a tour of the Forbidden City, which was off limits to all but the emperor's friends, family and staff but since Communism took over it had become a tourist trap. Compared to what we have in Washington, DC it was humble, but it was the best the Chinese could come up with.

While walking past the Chinese Parliament building I noticed a giant digital clock, the numbers must have been at least ten feet high. I noticed it was counting down and by the time left on the clock I could guess what it meant, but I asked just to make sure. "That is the time remaining until we take back Hong Kong." Britain was supposed to have Hong Kong in perpetuity but they decided to be civilized and hand control of Hong Kong, Kowloon and the New Territories back to China at the end of the New Territories 99 year lease which ended on July 1, 1997. Jokingly I said, "Where is the clock for Taiwan?" knowing this was a still a bit of a sore spot for China's ego. My host looked at me intently and said, "WE GO TOMORROW!" Sorry I mentioned it, sheesh!

The next day we took a taxi up to The Great Wall of China where I saw my first Kentucky Fried Chicken in China. Amazing how widely the fruits of American capitalism have spread. It was a sight to see a plastic statue of Colonel Sanders standing outside a KFC within view of the Great Wall of China.

To get to the top of the wall where you can really enjoy it we had to take a tram. While standing in line to get onboard the tram I noticed a long piece of steel cable that looked like it had snapped sometime in the past. It was frayed and unwound along its length. My host noticed me looking at it and perhaps noted that I had a worried look on my face. She tried to reassure me by saying, "Don't worry, built by the French!" Oh gee, I sure feel better about that, not much though because I know the French too. I've seen their work and they aren't much better. They made the analog in the S9000 tester. It still had pots you had to tweak when everyone else had gone to auto-cal. Just start the program and come back in a couple of hours. TA-DA!

To thank us for our work at Beijing the ABOM people told us they would take us out to lunch at a local restaurant. Fred hadn't eaten lunch since he found that shard of metal in his box lunch, so he was happy that he would finally be able to get something edible, or so he thought. We walked to the restaurant expecting something other than what we came across. We found ourselves in a shack with a dirt floor and were led through the kitchen which looked more like a pet store. The dirt floor had cages full of animals stacked up to five high. I recognized a few of the animals, snakes, chickens, ducks, and other things I didn't recognize. We were led to a banquet room and wined and dined as best as these people could do. It was far more disgusting than anything we had seen in Taiwan, but Fred and I ate anyway, not wanting to offend our customers and hosts. We figured if we drank enough Tsingtao beer everything would at least get sterilized in our stomachs, our poor livers would revolt later I expect, but I would rather die of liver failure later than of some godawful disease now.

Since we had finished up in Beijing it was time to go to Shanghai to visit another ABOM installation. Shanghai was a very interesting place, mostly because of the influence of The Bund, a row of old colonial buildings on the Huangpu River that were built by several European nations to allow them to run shipping from Europe up the river to Shanghai and back. The Bund was off limits to everyday Chinese until just recently, so like the Forbidden City it was a huge draw for tourists from both China and visitors around the world.

One evening we were walking along the Huangpu River shoreline and I had filled up on enough TsingTao beer that I needed to relieve myself very badly. Unlike the U.S., most of the world has almost no public restroom facilities. In Germany I had seen old men cupping their penises, palm down to hide the fact they were pissing into the bushes in the middle of a downtown area and little kids being held over the gutter in the street to defecate. The same was true here in China, almost no public bathrooms but it was not allowed to relieve yourself in public. The fine was apparently monstrous and there were enough of those armed (no bullets) Red Army guys around that they would catch you. We rushed down the walk looking for the nearest public restroom and finally found one, but you had to pay. I didn't have the right kind of money, being a foreigner, but one of my hosts paid for me and I barely made it. Whew! Gotta learn to drink less beer when I'm in China!

We finally had to go to work, but at least our trip was near the end. We visited the Shanghai ABOM facility and got signed in. This building was a little bit newer but it seemed to be quite cold inside. I was told that the government had a law that said that buildings south of the Huangpu River could not be heated, since it was costly to make enough electricity to heat all those homes and buildings for the millions upon millions of people. I noticed another make-work crew moping the concrete floors with buckets of dirty water. I found myself thinking the floor is never going to dry at these temperatures. What really worried me is that the testers are not supposed to experience large temperature swings. Electronic circuitry changes characteristics when the temperature changes and these guys had a habit of turning the systems off when they weren't being used. All over the world these systems are kept on continuously to keep them at a constant temperature. Here they didn't have the power to keep them powered up. So now the systems are at about 40 degrees F and we have to turn them on and let everything warm up for at least an hour before we get to do anything with them.

I figured I would at least the get the test programs loaded on the system and compiled, but I found the compiler wasn't there, the Make command just issued a warning that said, "Compiler Not Found." I couldn't believe it! How could you lose the Pascal compiler? This site only had one tester and they could not find the backup tapes that came with the system so now I was in real trouble. I decided I needed to call a tech support guy in the States and figure out what to do.

That was easier said than done, because at the time there were almost no telephones in China. To find one we had to go to another building, which was a problem because the best way to fix a problem is to have someone in Tech Support walk you through the process while you typed things on the computer keyboard. That wasn't going to work here because the tester was a long way away from the only phone we could use, and we had to mount quite a campaign to even use that one phone because of the cost of calling overseas.

Finally they relented and I got in touch with Will Charlatan in the States who told me how to fix the problem. Apparently the Chinese engineers had not deleted the compiler, but had deleted the compiler license. Will was able to find the code that would enable the compiler again. I wrote it down, went back to the building where the tester was, walked down the still wet hallway floor and got the system up and running. At the end of the day all was well, except the floor that was still wet, it had been all day. Oh, but here came the night crew to mop it again. Imagine working in a building where the floor is perpetually wet over the whole winter. Insanity!

Back at the hotel, the Sheraton no less, Fred and I went to the bar to get a drink, but right away we realized we had picked the wrong place. Three Chinese girls surrounded us, followed us across the room and sat down on a couch with us. One of the girls started stroking my beard and telling me how *pretty* I was. "Where's the toilet?" I asked. They pointed, I got up and bolted for the door. I was shocked! I thought a Sheraton would have more class than that. So I went to the front desk to complain. They told me that the fourth floor bar was *prostitute free*, I had simply gone into the wrong bar. Oh, well, that explains it all!

We flew back to Hong Kong and basked in the relative plenty of the brand new airport on Lantu Island, complete with a Burger King where Fred and I ravenously gobbled down the first good meal of our two week trip. We were elated to be out of there, and I was shocked at how much Fred complained about our two week adventure. Being Asian, I thought he might be more forgiving, but on the contrary, he berated the whole place mercilessly. He reminded me that he had grown up in Hawaii, there is no place in Hawaii that is anywhere **near** that bad! I guess I hadn't thought of that. I was just glad to have him with me, it would have been unbearable without Fred.

I never went back to China, but poor Fred did. Some more test programs needed to be delivered, more training had to be done. My side of things were handled by a guy named Mike Voitz who I trained on the tester years ago. According to Fred, that trip didn't go very well. Fred and Mike didn't really get along, and he made my day by telling me how much he missed my company on that trip. I like Fred a lot but I wasn't going to go to China again just to hold his hand and commiserate with him. I was done with China, thank God!

A couple of years later an article appeared in the print magazine Popular Science about China's Aerospace, Ballistics and Ordinance Ministry. I read in disbelief the gushing accolades the author bestowed on China's ABOM which he compared favorably to NASA. I was stunned that a gullible reporter could be so easily taken in by such incompetent boobs. I dashed off a letter to the editor of Popular Science very critical of the article and ABOM, doubting they would publish it. Popular Science published an earlier letter of mine chastising them for calling the Far Side of the Moon the "Dark Side of the Moon." The far side of the moon is bright for two weeks, just like our near side of the moon. I was getting tired of paying for a subscription to a magazine that was so full of hogwash and my letter critical of ABOM was a rather angry tirade.

A month or so later I was surprised to see that not only did they print my letter, they put it at the top of the Letters page with my name in big, bold print. Realizing that I had just imperiled Steppenwolf's reputation with this letter I decided to humble myself before my boss and offer my resignation for any embarrassment I caused the company, even though I had not mentioned Steppenwolf by name, thank God! My boss at the time, Lars Tarson read the letter and then told me not to worry about it. He had no plans to try to sell anything into China anyway, and if they did they would be sure not to send me. As Will Charlatan said, I would be *persona non grata* in China. I had just saved myself from any more travel to China, but nearly lost my job in the process. I would try to be more careful in the future. And then I wrote this book. Who says behavior isn't built into our DNA?

Gart: *Conductor! Conductor! Conduc--!*
Conductor: *You all right, Mister Williams?*
Gart: *Yeah, yeah. Sure, I'm all right. Willoughby. Next time -- next time, I'm going to get off. I'm going to get off at Willoughby.*
The Twilight Zone, A Stop At Willoughby by Rod Serling

Europe

"Ein Mass bitte!"

How to stay sane in Germany

Compared to Asia or even the U.S., traveling to Europe could be a treat, or a nightmare, depending on the customer you were servicing. My first trip to Europe was not to Europe proper, but rather to Ireland, home of the Blarney Stone, castle ruins and not much else. I had been traveling quite a bit in my new job at Steppenwolf Systems and had just found out I was scheduled to be teaching a class at LogAnaChip in Limerick. My wife April was visiting me at work one day when I introduced her to my boss, Mike Noyce who ran the Field Service operation at RadChek and now ran Field Service and Training at Steppenwolf. While April was there, Mike apologized to her for sending me all over the world recently (remember the Hong Kong->Rancho Bernardo fiasco) and asked her if there was anything he could do to make it up to her. Without missing a beat April (not being shy in the least) piped up and said, "I want to go to Ireland with Dan!" He was somewhat taken aback, but promised that he would look into it.

At the time, Steppenwolf travel policy stipulated that air travel over eight hours be done in Business Class, a rather civilized policy at the time. In addition, the policy allowed a spouse to travel with an employee in Coach Class in exchange for the single Business Class seat. Mike let me know that, yes, April could travel with me to Ireland. That meant we had to arrange for our three children to be taken care of, but their grandparents were only willing to take them for a week, and my training class ran two weeks. That was good enough for us. April would travel with me to London's Heathrow Airport, then on to Shannon International just outside of Limerick. The only hitch was that somehow I was booked into Business Class on the short flight from London to Shannon, and April had to sit in Coach, but that was no big deal.

At Shannon we picked up our rental car, a Volkswagen Polo which in the U.S. it would be called a Rabbit. Of course it was a right hand drive car with a manual transmission. April and I had both driven on the wrong side of the road in Australia, but neither of us had ever driven a stick-shift in a right hand drive car. After a few miles it became perfectly natural and we made our way to our hotel, Jury's in Limerick. Once we checked into the hotel we drove to the LogAnaChip plant to make sure we could find it before I had to start my class the next day on Monday. On the way we came across a car in the middle of a roundabout with an old man inside. We pulled over to see if we could help, as did many other folks. The old man was confused, shaken, and stunned by all the onlookers who were trying to figure out what to do to help. He exclaimed "Saints preserve us, they come out like angels all around!" Apparently this old gentleman had been driving on this road since he was a boy, but very recently Limerick had changed the intersection into a roundabout to comply with new directives from the EU to reduce crash deaths. This poor old guy was on virtual autopilot when this roundabout thrust itself into his world completely without warning. The EU, in an attempt to save lives had nearly taken one!

We walked around Limerick soaking up the atmosphere and looking for things to do. We found a Texas steakhouse for dinner. A magician worked the restaurant floor going table to table doing tricks for tips.

So after having a relaxing Sunday we began our daily grind. April would drop me off at the LogAnaChip plant where I would teach what little I knew of the tester I had been introduced to only a few months earlier, and she would drive our little Volkswagen all over Ireland exploring. However, that doesn't mean that I missed out on all the fun. This trip took place in late May, near Summer Solstice which meant it didn't get dark until 10PM. So April would pick me up at LogAnaChip at 5PM, then drive me all over to explore the countryside looking for castles, abbeys and graveyards in the area.

One place we found was so interesting that we went there twice. Carrigogunnell is the ruins of a castle that was blown to bits by the Dutch general Godert de Ginkell in the seventeenth century in the Williamitte War. While some portions of the castle remained standing, most of it was left laying on the ground, including massive stone spiral staircases. It was a beautiful place with a fantastic view of the Shannon River off in the distance. In addition we went to Blarney Castle where April kissed the Blarney Stone and Bunratty Castle where we dined medieval style complete with mead as the beverage.

On her own April, visited Waterford and Tipperary and abbeys and graveyards all over Ireland. We had one Saturday together and made it as far south as Cork, then back to the hotel to prepare for April's departure on Sunday morning. I dropped her off at Shannon the next day, watched her plane take off and then headed out on my own. Of course the mood was much different without her, very somber despite the wonderful scenery and artifacts including the Paulaborne Dolman on the Burren in County Clare.

After that my time in Ireland was rather boring, but I finished the class to the customer's satisfaction and took them out to eat a fancy celebratory dinner. While dining on the exquisite cuisine paid for by

Steppenwolf, the Irishmen told an endless stream of Irish sheep jokes to liven the mood. Like this — One Irishman says to another, "We all love to have our fun with sheep, but I wonder how other Irishmen do it?" The other Irishman says, "I just pick them up and drop their hind legs into my boots so they can't get away." The other Irishman says, "Yeah, but then you can't kiss them!" Sick, very sick!

A year or so later I was asked to give a class on a new tester that had been sold to a TerRants plant in Southampton England. The problem here was I needed to be trained before I could give a class on the tester, so my first stop was Boston, Massachusetts. I only had one glitch here, since my brain told me I was traveling in-country I left my passport at home, then had to ask my wife to Fed-Ex it out to me in Boston.

After spending a week getting up to speed on the new tester I flew to London's Heathrow airport and caught the airport bus out to the rental car lot. There, the gent running the lot got me to my car and opened the gate to let me out of the lot. I would have liked a few minutes to gather my thoughts and figure out the controls on this right-hand drive car, but the guy was holding he gate open, so off I went, driving into the heart of the biggest airport in the world. After looping around through this roundabout and that one, I finally made it onto M3 heading south.

I had been faxed directions but once I got to Southampton proper I got lost, very lost. I drove around for hours, asking for directions but it was no good. These people were all locals so they gave me landmarks like "turn left when you see Johnny's Scottish Terrier." Not very helpful. Finally I stumbled onto my hotel. Very relieved I checked in and took the tiny, tiny lift (elevator we call them) to my room. It was a decent place and they had an excellent restaurant with a complete breakfast menu including my new favorite, kippers and eggs. Yummy, but stinky!

On the second night, the fire alarm went off in the middle of the night. They locked off the elevator, so to get out of this six story building we all had to walk down the outside fire escape stairway. One old geezer was slowly making his way down, step by step. By the time he reached the ground, the fire department decreed it to be a false alarm so it was time to make our way back to our rooms. The lift was so small, it could only accommodate about four people at a time, so I decided to let the geezer have the lift, and I walked back up the fire escape stairs.

The class was given inside the TerRants plant in Southampton. The customers were all English, very pleasant, friendly people and one of them was wheelchair-bound. This wasn't really a problem until the end of the class when we had our final class lunch.

Southampton is on a pair or rivers, the River Test and the River Itchen, that combine into Thc Solent which allows boats to make the passage to the Isle of Wight. Occasionally I would go to the Town Quay where there was a shopping center and a couple of great restaurants overlooking the harbor and boat moorages. One Friday I was having dinner while I watched a young wife pack the kids, bags of groceries and sleeping bags into a sailboat for what appeared to be a weekend of sailing around the Isle of Wight. What a great life I thought.

That weekend I toured the countryside in my rented Vauxhall automobile. I went to see Stonehenge which was very, very impressive, but in a haunting, enchanting way. Much like the Vietnam War Memorial in Washington, DC. Sure, it's just a collection of rocks, but the people it represents reminded me of my heritage and my ancestors' great accomplishments.

Driving through the countryside I came across a castle that was being used as a filming location for the TV show Dr. Who. I didn't bother paying the fee to visit the site. Unlike Ireland where most of the castles were free, most English castles charge a hefty fee to enter, and by then I had my fill of castles. I also drove to Portsmouth, the port the Pilgrims departed from. Portsmouth had many tourist attractions including a replica of the first assembly line making blocks for sailing ships, and most impressive was the very ship that Lord Admiral Nelson commanded against the Spanish Armada, his flagship, the HMS Victory. Most amazingly they had removed the deck boards that Lord Admiral Nelson had died on and moved them inside the ship so that his blood would not be entirely washed away by the weather. So much history, so much to be proud of!

As we got closer to the end of the class, I needed to find a place for our class dinner and the Town Quay was my favorite spot to go, so I made reservations for the class there. Many of the pubs in England seemed to have the bar on the ground floor, and the restaurant on the "first floor." The first floor in England being the equivalent of the second floor in America. Problem was that we had the one wheelchair bound fellow, so I had to make sure they had a "lift" to get him up to the first floor. No worries, I know what I'm doing! It's only a foreign country, what could go wrong?

The day of our class lunch we arrived and left our friend on the ground floor to make his way to the lift. We waited for about 10 minutes, but he never turned up. We went back downstairs and found him sipping a drink.

The lift was out of order and instead of telling us they just gave him a complementary drink and left him there. Luckily there was another acceptable restaurant on the Quay so we paid for our drinks and made our way over there. Their lift did work, so we finally had a pleasant class lunch together. Whenever I ate with these guys I found that I was always the last one to finish eating. For some reason the English just wolf down their meals. No wonder the French, who savor meals over hours find the English uncivilized. After three weeks away from home I flew back to the States, mission accomplished again.

I never went back to Ireland or England, but I did make several trips to Germany and the low countries. My first trip to Germany was to teach a two week class at the Steppenwolf office in Munich. I arrived on Saturday and found a message waiting at my hotel from Ilsa Strudel, the wife of Randy Strudel who was in charge of the office in Munich. Ilsa was as American as I was but she fit into Germany like a local. Her note was an invitation to join her for a bicycle outing in the English Garden along with one of the German service guys, Wolfgang.

She picked me up at the hotel on Sunday morning and we drove back to her house where she explained that her husband, Randy was back in the States for a meeting, but she was under orders to take care of me in his absence. She lent me his bicycle and we met up with Wolfgang and rode all through the English Garden. We ate lunch at one of the outdoor cafes and drank a gallon of beer. German beer is the best, especially their Pilsner. You can keep the Hefeweizen, tastes too much like yeast to me. Let the Pils flow, "Ein Mass bitte!" which means give me a liter of beer, and make it snappy please! After a wonderful day I was told how to get to the Steppenwolf office and left to sleep it off at my hotel.

The next day I arrived several hours before class was scheduled to start so I could prepare. Ilsa was there to help out, even though she wasn't an employee she was helping make sure I would have a smooth start as the customers I was to be training were very important, and very, very smart.

As the students filed into the room I realized that I was going to have my work cut out for me. Each one presented his business card, and every one of them had at least a Master's degree, two of them had PhDs. I had no degree and no formal training in mixed signal, only what I had learned over the last year or so. This was going to be tough. As the class went on I found the Germans to be very competent and friendly people. They didn't berate me on any point, and when they made an inquiry I didn't know the answer to, I was able to figure it for them within a day or so. We also had two French guys in the class, they were good folks too, but there was a difference. Every day at lunchtime we would all go out to some local cafe to eat together. One time we went to a Chinese restaurant, the Germans and I asked for chopsticks, but the French refused to even consider such barbarity! Knife and fork s'il vous plait!

During another lunchtime outing we tried a nearby Greek place and enjoyed it so much that we went again the next week, but this time we brought along the stunningly beautiful office receptionist Heidi. This time we noticed a change in the proprietor's demeanor. Our first time there he had been a bit of a stodgy, old coot, but when we brought Heidi he lavished attention on us, even giving us two rounds of Ouzo on the house! It pays to travel with beautiful women!

By day I taught these German geniuses all I knew about the tester, by night I would roam the city riding the U-bahn or underground subway around Munich visiting places all over the city. Sometimes I would walk, but most times it was easier just to get on the U-bahn which was clean, safe and cheap. The only downside is that you don't get to see any of the city from underground, but Munich is a big place and driving there was out of the question for me. I was warned by Ilsa to be sure to buy a ticket for each ride on the U-bahn. Ilsa had once ridden with her dog. She had a ticket, but she failed to buy one for the dog. She got a citation for almost $200 U.S.!

I did have one strange experience on the U-bahn that got a little scary. I was standing on the station platform waiting for a train to make the next leg of my trip home. When the train arrived, everyone got off the train, which I thought was strange. There was some German message coming out of the loudspeakers, but I didn't understand it, so I just figured everyone was getting off at this stop. When I boarded the train, everyone on the platform looked at me like I was insane. Unlike China, Korea or other nonwhite countries, in Germany anyone who is white is assumed to be German, or at least smart enough to understand at least a little German. They all assumed I understood the announcement, "This train is being diverted to the maintenance area. Please disembark and wait for the next train." So after I got on the train, it disappeared into this dark underground area, and the lights in the train went off! They were going to park the train here and work on it tomorrow morning. Would I be able to get out and navigate my way through the tunnels without getting run over by a fast moving subway train?

Luckily there was an emergency call button on the train, so I pushed it. I'm sure the engineer was shocked that someone would be on the train. After I got him to speak English (bitte) I explained my situation. He came and got me and walked me to a passage that allowed me to get back to the platform to catch the next *in-service* train to my destination. *Whew!*

Germans are very rule oriented, and very much dislike foreigners who don't know, or don't follow the rules. However, that doesn't mean they were Puritanical in their beliefs. Far from it, they are the most sexually unrepressed people I have ever met. I was astonished when I came across my first "Sex Shop." In the U.S. we call these Adult Book Stores but in Germany they don't mess around. The Sex Shops were full of sex toys, pornography of all types including child porn, which was rather disturbing to this American. In the U.S. these shops are frequented by single men, but in Germany there were plenty of couples browsing the Sex Shops, getting advice from the salesperson on the effectiveness of this sexual aid versus that sexual aid, or just thumbing through the stacks of erotic magazines together. Perhaps getting some ideas for the evening's entertainment back home.

On the street (Strasse) there were very erotic advertisements for movies or other sexually explicit events right out in the open alongside ads for children's clothing or food stores. One showed the photo of a young teenage girl naked all the way to the waist, breasts and all. It was an advertisement for a film about an adult man who has an affair with a young girl. Young schoolboys walked past this ad without even noticing. In my youth, every boy in the neighborhood would have been glued to that ad for months on end.

In the end, I finished my class and the customers gave me very positive critiques. They also reported back to Randy Strudel, now back from his trip to the States how much they enjoyed my class. This gave me a huge boost in my career as I now had an advocate way up in the hierarchy of the company. Especially important, because later Randy Strudel became president of Steppenwolf Systems.

I made several trips to Germany, and became increasingly comfortable speaking German and increasingly familiar with German behavior overall. Once I arrived in Munich with a replacement circuit board and decided to go through the Customs Red Line where my cargo and paperwork would be scrutinized. The two German civil service workers were pretty upset that I ruined their day by bothering them. They were having a lovely day sitting around doing nothing until I showed up. "*Dummkopf*!" Compared to the Korean Customs officer who figured out I was smuggling a laptop into Seoul for the TestEz Korean rep, these guys were very laid back.

On another trip to Germany I was asked to also teach a two day class on a new software tool to a customer in Oudenaarde in Belgium. So after two weeks of teaching in Munich, I caught a plane to Brussels and was picked up by the local salesman, Ivan Petroff and his boss, Dick Carton. They drove me though the countryside to the little town where there was a small Seaman's manufacturing plant just outside of Oudenaarde.

This trip was memorable for two reasons. One, there wasn't any place to eat a decent meal in Oudenaarde! I had the choice of eating a full blown 3 hour French dinner at the hotel I was staying at, or I could walk into town and find a pub where the only food they served was twenty-four varieties of toast. No burger joints, no supermarkets, no cafes, nothing! I thought for sure I would starve to death in Oudenaarde.

The other reason this trip was memorable was that the customer was very keen on getting some changes made to this fancy new software tool, similar to the one I taught Dick Cadillac at Gizmotronics in Kokomo. They gave me a list of their suggested enhancements and wanted to know right away if they were going to get their wish list. That night I spent several hours trying to contact my coworker in the States, Ken Thomas who worked on this particular software package.

When I finally got through I was told that Ken had been laid off, and the project had been cancelled. *Just great,* I thought to myself, the customer is expecting upgrades to software they just recently bought, and now the project has been cancelled and the only person who knows anything about it has been laid off! What should I tell the customer? I hate lying, but Ivan advised me to just tell them I couldn't get through and that he would address their concerns later. I was happy to get out of Oudenaarde and I was rewarded with one more night in Belgium at a really spacious $250 a night hotel in Brussels. Finally some good food and a decent place to sleep!

A while later I was asked to go back to Germany to help with a problem at TIT in Freiburg near the German-French border on the Rhein River. I was paired up with a former coworker from San Jose by the name of Tim Homer. Tim had never been to Germany so I told him all about it before our trip, including all the details about the Sex Shops. We arrived at Munich and drove a rented Audi A4 down to Freiburg by way of the autobahn. Tim was a really good driver so despite this being his first trip he did an outstanding job getting us down there. We had a hotel on the top of a hill overlooking the town of Freiburg, it was a fantastic venue.

However, the customer made the trip a lot less fun. He was a manager by the name of Mister Hussein. Because TIT was a very important customer, everyone with any skills at all was sent to help me and Tim figure out this problem. On board was Gil Andrews from the University of

Errorladen who had worked on this problem for weeks without resolution, along with my old friend Hans Blecher. Hans could be hilarious at times. He was a very competent engineer with an accent that was an exact duplicate of the character Sigfreid on the TV sitcom *Get Smart*.

Gil kept thinking the problem that TIT was seeing was due to his STDF "datalogging" code. Tim, being a hardware guy was certain it was hardware problem. Hans and I reserved judgement. We worked as much as we could, but not as much as we would have liked because Germany has very strict labor laws. By law you are not allowed to work longer than 8 hours a day, 40 hours a week, and so we were stuck there until the problem was solved but had limited time to figure it out. In Asia or the U.S. I could put in 16 hours a day, and while grueling, it usually got the job done. In Germany, 8 hours was the max, and it was slowing us down considerably.

One day we worked all day on the hardware to placate Tim and left the tester put back together but didn't have time to run the auto-calibration, again, being constrained by the 8 hour rule. So we left the TIT guys to do the calibration hoping that the tester would be OK. It's not like they had to do much anyway, just dock the calibration station to the tester, start the auto-calibration program and walk away for a few hours.

That night after knocking back eight or so beers each, I put in a call to Ren Stimpson, the account manager back in Boston, so I could fill him in. He came unglued at the prospect of us leaving the tester in an unknown state overnight and told me to gather everyone up and go back to the plant. I went downstairs to the bar to deliver the unhappy news that our now very inebriated crew had to go back to work. They didn't take it very well. Hans, in a perfect impersonation of Sigfreid exclaimed "Vee are not horses!" Tim said, "No, horses get a rest occasionally!" OK boys, enough grazing, let's go.

So the four of us, almost too drunk to drive, piled into the Audi and drove over to TIT. We were told by the guards we would not be allowed to work, but one of us could go in and check on the tester. I drew the short straw so I went in. I was convinced by the TIT staff that the tester was running well and delivered the happy news back to my stinking drunk colleagues.

After a week or so we ruled out a hardware problem and decided that Gil's STDF code was not to blame, so Gil took Tim back to Munich and Hans and I stayed around to troubleshoot the problem.

One day sitting on the test floor, Hans and I were trying yet another experiment when Mister Hussein came up behind us and said, "If you guys were from DactylDyne (our competitor) you would have solved this problem already!" When he walked away Hans turned to me and said, "Zis Mister

Hussein, I really hate zis guy!" I nearly died laughing! Of course I had to keep it quiet because Mister Hussein hadn't gotten too far away from us and he would have known he was the butt of some offensive joke.

Eventually Hans had to go back home to Munich, and I was left alone to work on the problem. I got to know the bartender at the hotel bar, a very cute, young German woman. One evening I complained to her that the Pilsner glasses she was giving me were too small, I would like a larger glass, like the glasses that the Hefeweizen comes in. "Oh no, this is not allowed!" she exclaimed. There are laws for which beer goes into which glass. However, because we were alone, she relented, but told me that if someone entered the bar, she would grab my glass and dump it out to avoid getting in trouble with the law. See what I mean about Germans and rules?

Eventually I figured out what the problem was, but I couldn't prove it directly, nor could I solve it out here in the field. The test program was gobbling up computer memory and not releasing it at the end of a device test. So the more devices tested, the more memory the program gobbled up and eventually the poor computer ran out of memory and crashed.

It was a software problem that only a software engineer from the States could fix. I got permission to come home while my good friend Malcolm Reynolds, the only software engineer stupid enough to have a passport got on a plane to come to Germany. He used a program called Purify to pinpoint the problem. I was right, it was a memory leak, caused by a stupid error in the system software. Malcolm proved it and fixed it, much to TIT's and Mister Hussein's delight and everyone else's chagrin.

However now I had to get back to Munich by way of the autobahn. This would be my first time driving with no speed limits, and I had to do it on a Friday afternoon. After a while I got the hang of it but by the time I got to the Munich area it was dark and I kept getting lost! I needed to find the right exit so I could get to my hotel and get some sleep before my flight back to the States in the morning. I don't know how many times I drove past the exit for Dachau, site of an infamous Nazi concentration camp, but finally I got the right exit for my hotel, got some sleep and made my flight the next day.

On a later trip to Germany, I was sent over to represent Steppenwolf at a trade show, Semicon Europa that was being held at a new convention center built on the site of the old Munich airport that served as my first port of call to Germany. The new airport was built way outside of town and now they had extended the U-bahn all the way out there, so no more driving from the airport, just get on the train and go! Because Steppenwolf had acquired so many companies in the past few years and we had representatives from each of the product lines at the show, I would have plenty of U.S. compatriots to help me enjoy Germany.

Most of the time at the show was spent standing around, talking to customers and giving demonstrations. This was the first time my division did a demonstration without a tester on site, and it was my idea. Instead of shipping a tester all the way across the Atlantic, I had two testers setup back in Beaverton, Oregon that I could run remotely by way of the internet to show the speed improvement of the new product I was touting. It worked perfectly because daytime in Germany is very early in the morning in the U.S. I was assured that no one would be using the testers when I needed them because of the ungodly hour in Beaverton thanks to the time difference.

Two of the guys from San Jose hung out with me in our off time, Rick Dribas, a rather young guy who was new to the whole trade show thing, and Trig Harrison, an experienced marketing sales guy for one of the new products. One night we went to a famous, downtown Hofbrauhaus where Rick and Trig tried to walk out with a "mass" or a one liter beer mug. They were caught by the staff and their mugs were confiscated. From there I knew it would only get worse. Next, we caught a taxi to take us to one of the local "red light districts" so Trig could satiate his curiosity about the local brothels. Rick and I went along but once we got there Rick, whose wife had just had a baby got cold feet. The place was kind of a dive, and they didn't even know how to make a decent martini. They gave me vodka and sweet vermouth instead of dry vermouth. Hadn't these people ever seen a Bond flick before?

Once Rick and I realized this was not a good place to be for married men (ya think), the two of us decided to leave. The problem was the brothel staff locked the door, so when I did my now classic "Where's the bathroom" bolt for the door, the door was locked! The Madame kept asking us in German what we wanted. I just shouted "I want to go out and smoke!" Stupid of course, because they let you smoke inside a brothel, but that's all my beer addled brain could come up with. They let us out and we found a taxi to take us back to the hotel. The next day we learned Trig also decided to leave just a few minutes after we did, but after looking for us in vain he found his own taxi and made it back to the hotel. Likely story, Trig! Whatever, we were happy to be done with that evening!

One of the problems with European architecture is that they don't use carpet anywhere. At the show I found myself getting weary of standing on hard floors all day to the point I could hardly walk after a day at the show. By the end of the show, I had to lift my feet manually to get into a car to accompany Oskar Schmitt, the top sales guy in Germany on a trip to Freiburg to talk to TIT. Oskar is a great guy, and he owned this fantastic 500 series BMW. Instead of taking the Autobahn to Freiburg, we took a two lane road through the Black Forest. It was beautiful, but Oskar drove like a race car driver. I don't know if this was his normal mode of driving or if he was just trying to impress me, but I could swear we were nearly killed several times. Instead of driving all the way to Freiburg in one day we stopped at a little hunting lodge in the depths of the Black Forest. A roaring creek passed just a few feet from the hotel. The rooms were huge, with massive bathtubs and showers in each room. The bathroom alone was larger than my whole room at the Ichiban in Japan. A really great place for only $50 a night!

We completed our journey to Freiburg the next day, visited the customer (not Mister Hussein this time) and then made a trip to Stuttgart where we visited another customer who operated test facilities in a now disused underground Cold War bunker. Since the Berlin Wall had come down these facilities were very cheap and were being used for all kinds of things. In this case a cell phone chip testing facility because the rooms were impervious to external radio signals from TV, radio and cell phone towers. I ran into two of my old colleagues, Hackett and Ivan, who were now working for the competition, DactylDyne, but it was good to see them nonetheless. It had been several years since we had seen each other. Hackett is the one who told me how pleased the German customers of my first training class were. Without Hackett, I might never have known why Randy Strudel seemed to favor me throughout my career at Steppenwolf.

Finally back in Munich, it was time to go home. This was my fourth and final trip to Germany, and by this time my spoken German was getting very good. When I got to the airport I checked in using German, but that was a mistake because the woman behind the counter started rambling off a whole bunch of stuff in German so fast I couldn't understand her. I said, "Nein, nein, English bitte!" She smiled and said, "Sorry, but your German is very good!" I became so used to German that even to this day I think *nein* but internally translate to *no* when responding in the negative.

While at TestEz, I invented a new way to generate test signals for ISO14443 Smart Cards. You probably have a few in your wallet, they are now incorporated into most credit cards. My invention proved to be the only way to meet all the test requirements of that standard. Now we had to sell it, and there was a RotoMolded plant in East Kilbride, Scotland that was building smart card chips so we arranged a visit with them and flew out to Glasgow. Along with the local English sales guy, Michael, the project manager, Mort Valdez and I drove from Glasgow down to East Kilbride and met with the RotoMolded engineers at the plant. RotoMolded had been under enormous pressure to keep this plant open after closing another plant in Bathgate back in 2001. The guys here were doing their best to make sure they didn't lose their jobs, too.

I was the marketing guy and Mort was the project manager but for some reason Mort took it on himself to act like the marketing and sales guy. I gave a demonstration showing our new card worked and showed the tools we had on hand to generate the waveforms that were needed to test Smart Card chips. I was a bit miffed that Mort failed to mention that I was the inventor of the heart of our test solution. Here we were in front of a potential customer where you have the opportunity to boost your reputation by saying, "Hey, we brought the inventor of this technology with us! That's how much we value your business!" I've done that myself in several situations. It boosts the ego of the inventor and raises the stature of the audience, as though they deserve to meet a person with such high standing. Everyone likes to be in the company of a winner, and patent holders are, by definition winners.

So Mort and I had a rather tempestuous relationship at this point. I'm not really sure why he brought me, but there I was, in Scotland. We spent a couple of days there, then headed back to Glasgow and ate a delicious Indian dinner served to us by a waiter who was clearly Indian, but spoke with a very distinctive Scottish accent. Very, very strange!

We spent the night in a local hotel and the next day left way early to head to the airport. Travel was getting increasingly difficult since September 11, 2001, and it was prudent to get to the airport many hours before the flight just in case. While standing in line at the ticket counter waiting to check in, Mort and I were discussing terrorism. He seemed to be sympathetic (with emphasis on pathetic) to the terrorists. I of course am pro-American all the way, and this caused a layer of friction between us.

Mort asked if I had heard about Daniel Pearl, the Jewish American who was beheaded just the day before. I had not heard the news so he showed me the front page of the local newspaper. The article upset me and soured our relationship even more. Let's not forget, part of the reason that we had to go to the airport so early is because of a terrorist attack that affected Lockerbie Scotland in 1988 when a Muslim man put his wife and child on Pan Am flight 103 with a bomb in her suitcase. How could you have sympathy for a guy like that?

Ever since that event, whenever you checked in, the airport personnel would ask you if you had let your bag out of your sight. Well, yeah! Sometimes we would check out of the hotel and leave our bags with the front desk, go visit a customer and then swing by the hotel to pick up our bags on the way to the airport. Even if we kept them with us, the bags would go in the trunk of the cab, where I can't see what's happening. Yeah, sure, their might be a midget terrorist in the trunk putting a bomb in my suitcase, but I doubt it. If you answered "Yes" you were in for a major search and hassle, but if you had a bomb in your suitcase, you and 400 other people were sure to die, so it was a tough call sometimes to lie to the airline and hope your suitcase wouldn't kill hundreds of people.

Then, off to the left of us came a security officer. I was certain he was coming for me, but instead he grabbed Mort and took him away for "additional security screening." Had they been listening in on our conversation? Had they used his pro-Islam arguments to select him for additional screening? He was half Asian, perhaps racial profiling had contributed to him being taken away. Who knows, but it was a wonderful case of *Schadenfreude* (German for taking pleasure in someone else's misfortune) and I relished watching him be dragged out of the check-in line and really happy it wasn't me!

I checked in wondering if I would ever see Mort again. Now I had over two hours to kill, what to do? I still had my DVD player so I found a quiet spot in the Glasgow airport and put the movie Gladiator in and watched the whole thing. I just love this movie and it was so appropriate for the topic Mort and I had been discussing. Besides, Hadrian's Wall was just 50 miles from where I was sitting. In fact, on our way to East Kilbride the salesman noted that we were driving over a bridge built by the Romans. The Romans had been here two thousand years ago!

Knowing the flight would be boarding soon I thought I should grab something to eat. I was so happy to find a Burger King in the Glasgow airport and bought my favorite, a Double Whopper and went looking for a place to sit down. Mort was there too and waved me over. I sat down and we had a pleasant chat. This time he was a bit more humble, having been given a thorough *going over* as they say.

Then Mort sheepishly brought up a topic that he thought would make me angry. He had bought an upgrade to Business Class and was afraid that I would be upset that he would be in Business while I was in Coach. However, this didn't bother me at all. I was happy for him. He paid for it out of his own pocket, I didn't, so what's the problem? Remember, I had flown in First Class with my Korean rep in Coach Class, and I had hoped that didn't bother him!

First Class boards first of course, then Business, and Mort said, "See you on the plane" and boarded. The call for "All rows" came and I made my way onto the plane. While walking through Business Class I could see Mort and he spotted me. Then suddenly a familiar face came into view. It was my old friend and travel agent from my Steppenwolf days, Bonnie Jell! Right in full view of Mort she gave me a big deep hug. We talked about what a coincidence it was to run into each other in a place like Glasgow. Then I said jokingly, "Bonnie, is it too late to get me an upgrade!" No, she couldn't and I really didn't expect her to, but I had hoped Mort heard me. I could prove I wasn't such a bad person, I got a hug on a plane in Glasgow from someone who was to him a total stranger. It was so great to see Bonnie after all these years. How many First Class upgrades had she gotten me in the past? How many times had I eaten caviar while looking down at the Aleutian Islands from 40,000 feet thanks to her? We said our goodbyes and I made my way back to my seat in Coach.

We arrived in Chicago, made it through Customs and then again, I met Mort and we had lunch together. Chicago-O'Hare is always a mess and this day was no exception. All the flights were late. He was flying to San Jose, Bonnie and I were flying to Portland, but our flight was only one hour late, Mort's flight was going to be at least three hours late. Again, more Schadenfreude. I'm sure Bonnie and I made it home before he did.

When the evening falls
And the daylight is fading,
From within me calls
Could it be I am sleeping?
For a moment I stray,
Then it holds me completely
Close to home - I cannot say
Close to home feeling so far away
Evening Falls by Enya

Epilogue - Escape to Willoghby

"This is Gart Williams, age thirty-eight, a man protected by a suit of armor, all held together by one bolt. Just a moment ago, someone removed the bolt, and Mr. Williams' protection fell away from him and left him a naked target. He's been cannonaded this afternoon by all the enemies of his life. His insecurity has shelled him, his sensitivity has straddled him with humiliation, his deep-rooted disquiet about his own worth has zeroed in on him, landed on target, and blown him apart. Mr. Gart Williams, ad agency exec, who, in just a moment, will move into the Twilight Zone - in a desperate search for survival."

Rod Serling's introduction to the episode "A Stop At Willoughby"

In 2005, someone removed **my** bolt, my armor flew off and I was left naked and vulnerable to every spear, bullet and arrow. I don't know quite what it was, although I suspect it had to do with the fact that I spent half a year traveling to San Jose every week to win one customer, but I had endured enough! Enough travel, enough time away from the wife and kids, enough filthy airplanes, enough filthy hotel rooms, enough filthy taxi cabs, enough 15 hour flights over the Pacific, the Atlantic, over the North Pole and over endless miles of farm fields in flyover country. I wanted out, and I was going to find my Willoughby.

The wife was with me. We had to get out of debt, I had to get a job that didn't require travel, even if I had to take a huge pay cut. We had to find a way to get off this rat race and leap off the train at Willoughby, no matter what the cost. Our son was nearly done with college which I had been paying for with cash out of my salary. We had a plethora of toys; boats, a yacht, a floating home, motorcycles, a hot tub, and of course our 2300 square foot house in Aloha, Oregon with all the amenities including two mortgages. It all had to go and we had to find someplace else to live, and live cheap.

We had been looking for something like a floating home, but more mobile because we found there was no sense in sitting in a marina jammed between other floating homes with neighbors we might, or might not get along with. In a regular land based house, you can handle a neighbor you don't like with a fence or wall, but in a floating home community, you are virtually wall to wall with your neighbors and you never know who is going to move in next door. That and the ever present threat of the State coming along and shutting down the marina leaving you with a house, but no place to live, as happened with *Darkwater Keep* at another Washington marina. We were going to make sure **that** never happened to us again.

We had been going to boat shows to see if we could find a yacht we could stand living on. In 2005 we attended the Seattle Boat Show on Lake Union on the week of our twenty-sixth wedding anniversary. We took the train, it was lovely. We looked at a lot of boats, big and small and finally came across a houseboat built by Catamaran Cruisers of Columbia, Tennessee. The twelve foot wide, 40 foot long houseboat looked intriguing. They made bigger versions too, up to 60 feet long. We thought why not put this maker on the list of places we might want to buy as a live-aboard boat?

We decided to use some of my Frequent Flyer miles to fly First Class to visit the factory and see if this boat would do the job, if this might be our Willoughby. At first I was skeptical. Then we took the factory tour with the sales guy. Wow, we were stunned. They seemed to know what they were doing. They offered a 50 foot model that was 14 feet wide and contained everything we would need. Two bedrooms, a bathroom, kitchen and living room, front deck, back deck, and upper deck. It was equipped with the same appliances in your typical motor home; gas and electric refrigerator with freezer, gas water heater, gas stove, gas furnace, 12 volt lights and other appliances. *This could work.*

We flew home and in a few days made the decision. We would name our boat *Great Ambition* as a lyrical version of a line from *A Stop At Willoughby*. You see, once Gart gets home after being blown apart and gets a glimpse of Willoughby, "A place where a man can slow down and live his life full measure" as the train conductor says, he has it out with his shrill, money grubbing wife. After he explains that he's sick and tired of running through his life at full throttle, his wife scolds him for his fantasy of living in an older, simpler time. She tells him: "It's my bad luck pal, my error, my miserable error to be married to a man whose **big dream** in life is to play Huckleberry Finn!" Big Dream became *Great Ambition*. I'd been screwed enough. I had excelled all over the world and been punished severely for it. What had it gotten me? Another plane ticket to some crappy place where I could spend my nights alone crying in my beer. That was it! No more armor, no more bolts, no more being a slave to a gaggle of creditors making money off my appetites for this toy or that toy or a bigger house or fancier cars.

We pulled the trigger in February of 2006 and got to work getting rid of everything we could. We sold our floating home and even made a profit. We ditched all the crap we accumulated over the years. I went looking for a new job. I had grown my hair out in protest of all the travel I had been doing.

Now I got a haircut and my old buddy, Red Stevens, told my boss Mick, “Dan got a haircut, I think that means he’s looking!” Mick flew up to have a talk with me. I told him straight out, he had promised me 20% travel maximum and I was doing better than 50%. He said he had no use for someone who couldn’t or wouldn’t travel. That clinched it.

We sold or gave away everything. I worked like a dog every night after work to fix up our Aloha house, nearly empty now that all the kids had moved out. I got an offer from Traxite in Hillsboro, Oregon with a recommendation from Rod Reardon, the director of test in San Jose that I had been flying down every week to impress.

TestEz tried to keep me, but I was done with them. The CEO called and begged me to stay, promising that I would never travel unless he decided it was necessary. I didn’t believe him. I thought, what good is that promise? You could tell me to get on a plane tomorrow. I just don’t want the threat of travel over my head ever again.

Finally we sold everything, even the house. We took our cash and ordered the boat, custom built to our specifications. We moved into a short term apartment near Traxite and waited for the boat to be built and trucked out from Tennessee. Eventually she arrived, she was just what we wanted. She was a huge houseboat with twin 115HP Yamaha outboards, indoor helm station and 4KW genset. Later we added RADAR, DirecTV auto-tracking sat dish, GPS, marine radio, solar power and a watermaker.

We made an agreement with the owner of the marina where our floating home *Darkwater Keep* had been, and still was, now with its new owner. We could live aboard at their marina and we could come and go as we pleased. They would provide us power, water and a place to pump out our black water tank. We got a storage unit in town for the last few things we couldn’t part with, complete with a mailbox.

We had some problems. Traxite decided that I should be transferred to either Dallas, Phoenix or San Jose, or take a layoff. I called April and asked her opinion. Without missing a beat she said, “Take the layoff. Will you be home for lunch?” A few days after I told Rod I would take the layoff, Traxite rescinded the ultimatum and reassigned me to another manager. However, I liked working for Rod a lot and wasn’t crazy about working for a company that would give me an ultimatum like that so I just quit. Since I didn’t have a mortgage or any other debt, I didn’t need another job, so we took four years off, touring the Columbia River in *Great Ambition* and loving every minute of it.

I had to look for work again to allow us to make a major modification to the houseboat. We added a third pontoon down the middle to make the boat stronger, ride higher and last longer. To make that happen I went to work for TerroDacNix. I made enough money to pay for the $30,000 upgrade, stuffed some more money in the bank and then got laid off, for the first time in my whole career. It was almost perfect timing!

Now all is well. We live a beautiful life floating on the Columbia River. We sit on the front deck and watch the Bald Eagles soar overhead, the River Otters play and chase fish in the river and the deer swim to the nearby island. We swim in the clean, cold water of the Columbia, walk the Columbia's pink and gray sand beaches, build beach bonfires and watch the twilight fade to an inky black star filled sky.

Because April raised our kids right even with me being gone half the time, we have grandkids. Occasionally they visit and we spend our time teaching them boating skills, giving them swimming lessons in our in-dock swimming pool and showing them how to live a good life on the river.

I work when I want, or not as I choose and we have enough to live on. I volunteer at the local library, help friends and neighbors and even complete strangers with technical issues. For fun and profit I create videos, write web pages, blogs, magazine articles and books.

Unlike most retired people I have **no desire to travel**. Why waste my own money traveling the world when I have already seen all I can stand? As you have seen, April got to accompany me on quite a few trips and has no desire to go anywhere else. We watch the planes go in and out of PDX with no desire to climb aboard another one.

I have been semiretired since 2009. We do what we want, spend every night in the same bed and every day together. Our love has never been stronger, and after what I have been through I would just a soon die as be separated from my wife. Never again, never. I've had my fill of the world and I have arrived at Willoughby.

34671141R00086

Made in the USA
San Bernardino, CA
03 June 2016